Read, America! Collection Selection

BEING YOUR BEST

Character Building for Kids 7-10

Barbara A. Lewis

Edited by Marjorie Lisovskis

free spirit
PUBLiSHiNG®

Works
for kids®

Library of Congress Cataloging-in-Publication Data

Lewis, Barbara A., 1943–
    Being your best : character building for kids 7–10 / Barbara A. Lewis ; edited by Marjorie Lisovskis
        p. cm.
    Includes index.
    Summary: Text, anecdotes, and activities introduce and discuss how to build important character traits, such as caring, citizenship, cooperation, courage, fairness, honesty, respect, and responsibility.
    ISBN 1-57542-063-5 (pbk.)
    1. Personality development—Juvenile literature. 2. Character—Juvenile literature. [1. Character. 2. Values. 3. Conduct of life.] I. Lisovskis, Marjorie. II. Title.

BF723.P4 L47 2000
155.2—dc21

            99-041180

At the time of this book's publication, all facts and figures cited are the most current available; all telephone numbers, addresses, and Web site URLs are accurate and active; all publications, organizations, Web sites, and other resources exist as described in this book; and all have been verified. The author and Free Spirit Publishing make no warranty or guarantee concerning the information and materials given out by organizations or content found at Web sites, and we are not responsible for any changes that occur after this book's publication. If you find an error or believe that a resource listed here is not as described, please contact Free Spirit Publishing. Parents, teachers, and other adults: We strongly urge you to monitor children's use of the Internet.

Ideas from the "Make Games More Fair" activity on pages 62–63 are adapted from *Playing Smart: A Parent's Guide to Enriching, Offbeat Learning Activities for Ages 4–14* by Susan K. Perry (Minneapolis: Free Spirit Publishing, 1990) and used with permission. The suggestions on pages 143–144 for finding or designating a safe house or block parent are adapted from *Bullies Are a Pain in the Brain* by Trevor Romain (Minneapolis: Free Spirit Publishing, 1997) and used with permission.

Photo credits: p. 17—Kym Meehan; p. 28—Linda Burnside; p. 41—Janice Johnson; p. 53—Sonja Balic; p. 64—Neskowin Valley School; p. 77—Calletana Montes; p. 90—Liz Zirkle; p. 107—Sowan Bahk; p. 120—Dawn Little; p. 136—Rodney Murdoch.

Cover and interior design: Marieka Heinlen
Illustrations: Albert Molnar
Assistant editor: Darsi Dreyer

10 9 8 7 6 5

Printed in the United States of America

Free Spirit Publishing Inc.
217 Fifth Avenue North, Suite 200
Minneapolis, MN 55401-1299
(612) 338-2068
help4kids@freespirit.com
www.freespirit.com

The following are registered trademarks of Free Spirit Publishing Inc.:
FREE SPIRIT®
FREE SPIRIT PUBLISHING®
SELF-HELP FOR TEENS®
SELF-HELP FOR KIDS®
WORKS FOR KIDS®
THE FREE SPIRITED CLASSROOM®

free spirit
PUBLISHING®
Works for kids®

Dedication

To Sam, who has always had a soft heart.

Acknowledgments

My thanks to Judy Galbraith, my publisher and friend, who continues to believe in me, and who sees the whole picture. Thanks to Margie Lisovskis and Caryn Pernu, my patient and caring editors. Special thanks to the whole Free Spirit staff, who fit themselves together like pieces of a jigsaw.

I am indebted to Kristie Fink, Supervisor of Character Education, Utah State Office of Education, for editorial help and for always exemplifying what she preaches.

My gratitude to those who shared stories: The Giraffe Project; Anne Voight at the U.S. Department of Justice; Kids for Saving Earth Worldwide; my friend, Helen Schmidt; and Linda Frost.

My deep appreciation and love to my dear husband, Larry; our children, Mike, Michelle, Andrea, Chris, and Sam; and our grandchildren, Skyler, Jordi, and Drew, for constant creative inspiration.

Table of Contents

List of Reproducible Pages

What's Character, and Why Do People Need It?

"I still want what I've always wanted . . . to be the best person I can be."

—Oprah Winfrey

Have you ever heard someone say, "You can't judge a book by its cover"? What this means is that you can't tell what happens in a book without reading all the words inside. Sometimes the cover only shows a small part of what happens in the story. Sometimes it really isn't much like the story at all.

Now think about *you*. Are you like that book? When people see the *outside* you, do they know everything about you? No, they don't. You have thoughts and feelings inside. Looking at the outside, people can't see what's in your mind and heart. They'd be mistaken if they thought they knew.

Have you ever had a teacher with a stern face who seemed unfriendly at first? Then, when you got to know her, you learned she was a very friendly, caring person inside? Her "cover" was different from the way she was inside.

This book is about the inside you—your **character.** Character means having positive qualities like caring, fairness, honesty, respect, and responsibility. We call these qualities **character traits.** This book can help you discover the positive qualities inside you. It can help you learn how to make them stronger.

What would it be like if people didn't share? If they weren't kind or honest? If they couldn't work together? If they didn't follow laws and rules? The world would be a pretty mean and lonesome place. That's one reason we have rules for living together. Strong character helps people follow the rules. But there's more to it than that. When you're caring, honest, and responsible, people respect you more. Best of all, you respect and feel proud of *yourself.* Just think about how good it feels when you share, treat someone kindly, tell the truth, or finish a job or chore.

There are many character traits you can develop. In this book, we'll talk about ten of them: *caring, citizenship, cooperation, fairness, forgiveness, honesty, relationships with family and friends, respect, responsibility,* and *safety.* (If you're not sure right now what each of these traits is, don't worry— you'll find out as you read.)

You don't have to be perfect. Developing strong character traits isn't easy. It takes a lifetime of courage and hard work. Now is a good time to start that work, and this book will help you. Think of it as your guide to becoming the very best person that you can be!

How to Use This Book

Being Your Best is about character. The first chapter asks you to think about yourself. What is your character like? What's important to you? How well do you know yourself? Short checklists help you to decide which character traits to work on first.

Each of the remaining chapters helps you think about one positive trait. At the beginning of every chapter is a true story about a kid (or kids) who had an important experience with that character trait. You'll meet children of different ages, backgrounds, beliefs, interests, and talents. Some of them did amazing things—like Lawrence Champagne III, who saved a busload of kids. Others did kind acts—like Kanesha Sonee Johnson, who helped her classmates get along better, or Zach Zirkle, who stood up to bullies to save his brother.

Following each story, you'll read a short section that tells about the character trait in more detail. Within the chapter, you'll find quotes to get you thinking. Definitions and other background information help you understand more about the trait and why it's important. Words you need to know are highlighted in **bold** type the first time they're used, and they're explained in the chapter where they're introduced. They're also defined in the glossary (pages 153–155). As you continue reading, use the glossary to check or recheck the meaning of words.

The chapters offer ideas for you to think and talk about. Each includes a section called "What If?" which describes situations where the best choice isn't always clear. Take some time to think about these situations. You might also want to write about them, talk about them with friends and family, or even **role-play** them (act them out). They'll help you learn more about developing good character.

When you talk about the "What If?" situations with other people, it might help to keep these guidelines in mind:

- **First, get the facts.** Have someone read the situation out loud. Then summarize what you all heard.
- **Listen to everyone's ideas.** Ask questions if you don't understand.
- **Borrow and build on other people's ideas.** This isn't stealing ideas—it's making them stronger. For example, if someone says, "I think the girl should talk to her teacher," someone else might say, "To the teacher or another grown-up."
- **Disagree respectfully.** Name-calling, put-downs, and bad language aren't respectful. You might say, "I understand what you mean, but maybe this would work better."
- **Remember that sometimes there might be more than one right answer.**

Each chapter has three or four activities you can do to build and practice the trait you're learning about. You'll also learn where to find books, Web sites, and organizations with more information about the traits.

You might decide to work on one character trait for a day, a week, or a month. Maybe you'll work on the traits in order, or maybe you'll jump around. Or you might dip into the book and read the parts that interest you the most. It's up to you.

I'd like to know how *Being Your Best* has helped you. Like the children in this book, you might have a story to tell. If you want to share it, please write to me:

Barbara A. Lewis
c/o Free Spirit Publishing
217 Fifth Avenue North, Suite 200
Minneapolis, MN 55401-1299

OR

Email address:
help4kids@freespirit.com

Web site:
www.freespirit.com

GETTING TO KNOW YOU

"You are your most valuable asset. Don't forget that.
You are the best thing you have."

—Gary Paulsen

When you look in a mirror, you see your outside self. What do you see when you look *inside* yourself? Maybe you see someone who's often kind, fair, friendly, and responsible. Maybe you see someone who can sometimes be crabby, or selfish, or forgetful. Or maybe you see someone with a little bit of both kinds of traits. Whatever you see, it's important for you to do two things:

1. Accept and like who and what you are. You know you're not perfect. Nobody is! You also know you have lots of good qualities. You can value yourself for the unique person that is *you*. To do this, you may want to learn about some of the things that make you a special person.

2. Work to develop stronger character "muscles." Your body needs strong muscles to help you walk, run, climb, jump, or lift. Character traits are like muscles. They can help you be more responsible, make good choices, and get along with other people. You can work to make your character muscles stronger. As you do, you might see some changes in your relationships. Maybe you'll begin to get along better with your friends, family, and teachers. You might start to make new friends. You'll probably do better in school. Most important, you'll feel better about yourself.

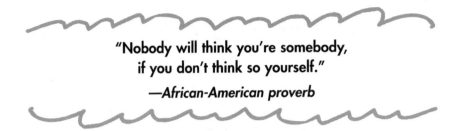

"Nobody will think you're somebody,
if you don't think so yourself."
—*African-American proverb*

Start by Quizzing Yourself

Each of the next ten chapters of this book shows you ways to build your character muscles. Before you start, take some time to get to know who you are and what you're like today. On pages 7–11 are four quizzes you can give yourself. The quizzes aren't hard—in fact, they're fun—and there are no wrong answers. You can use the quizzes to discover things

about the *inside* you. You'll learn about your beliefs and feelings, your relationships, and your interests, talents, and dreams. Every quiz tells what page to look at to learn what your answers mean. After taking each quiz, read that explanation. Think about what it means for you. Use what you learn to help you decide which character trait you want to work on first.

My Character Muscles

Copy this page. Read each pair of sentences. Check the ONE from each pair that describes you. Or check BOTH if you believe that you already have that trait but would like to make it stronger. **To learn what your answers mean, see page 12.**

1. _____ I'm kind and I care about helping others.
   _____ I'd like to be more kind and caring.

2. _____ I'm a good citizen. I like to help in my school, family, and community.
   _____ I want to be a better citizen. I want to help more in my school, family, or community.

3. _____ I take turns and cooper-ate with others.
   _____ Sometimes I don't like to take turns or cooperate with others.

4. _____ I'm fair with others, and I'm willing to share.
   _____ I usually only treat people fairly if I like them. I don't like to share.

5. _____ I forgive people easily.
   _____ It's hard for me to forgive people. Sometimes I hold a grudge.

6. _____ I tell the truth most of the time.
   _____ I often tell lies.

7. _____ I get along with my family and friends.
   _____ I argue and fight sometimes.

8. _____ I'm polite and I show respect for everyone.
   _____ Sometimes I interrupt, act rude, call people names, or make fun of people.

9. _____ I'm responsible. I do my chores and homework.
   _____ I don't always do my chores and homework.

10. _____ I play safely and try to keep myself and others safe.
    _____ I don't always play safely. Sometimes I take dangerous risks.

From *Being Your Best: Character Building for Kids 7–10* by Barbara A. Lewis copyright © 2000.
Free Spirit Publishing Inc., Minneapolis, MN: 800/735-7323; *www.freespirit.com.*
This page may be photocopied for individual, classroom, or group work only.

My Family and Friends

Copy this page. For each sentence, check the box that best describes how you feel about your relationships.
To learn what your answers mean, see page 13.

	Most of the time	Some of the time	Never or hardly ever
1. My friends like me.			
2. I like my friends.			
3. My parent(s) or guardian(s) listen to me when I talk.			
4. I listen to my parent(s) or guardian(s) when they talk to me.			
5. My friends have fun with me.			
6. I like my teacher(s).			
7. My teacher(s) like me.			
8. I like my brother(s) and sister(s). They don't bug me very much.			
9. My family and I share chores and work together.			
10. I think all people are important.			
11. My friends admire me and can count on me.			
12. It's easy for me to talk to younger kids.			
13. Younger kids like me.			
14. I like to talk with older people.			
15. Older people like me.			

Count the number of checks in each column and write the numbers below.

Number of **"Most of the time"** responses: _____

Number of **"Some of the time"** responses: _____

Number of **"Never or hardly ever"** responses: _____

TOTAL: _____

What's My Personal Style?

Copy this page. Read the following descriptions. Check the ONE that sounds the most like you. **To learn what your answer means, see page 13.**

_____ **1. I like to be alone much of the time.** I like other people, but I mostly like to play by myself. I like to be the one to choose what I do and play. I like doing my own work more than working in a group. I have one or two best friends who I like to be with the most.

_____ **2. I like to be with people most of the time.** I like working in groups rather than working alone. I like to make choices in a group. I have many friends. I have best friends, but I like being with all of my friends. I often get bored when I'm alone.

_____ **3. I sometimes like to work in a group, but I also like to do my own work.** Sometimes I like to be alone with no one around but me. At other times, I like to play with a whole group of kids. I have friends and like being with them, but I don't mind being alone.

A Snapshot of Me

What you are on the outside and who you are on the inside combine to make up the real you. Copy and fill in these pages. Use extra paper if you need to. When you're done, you'll have a more complete picture of the person you are right now. Think of it as a snapshot of *you* today. **To learn what your answers mean, see page 14.**

Here's what I look like:
(Draw a picture of yourself here, or paste in a photo.)

1. Things I like about myself are: _____

_____

2. My best character traits are: _____

_____

3. Traits I want to make stronger are: _____

_____

4. For me, making and keeping friends is:

_____ mostly hard   _____ mostly easy   _____ sometimes hard and
                                                     sometimes easy

5. For me, getting along with my family is:

_____ mostly hard   _____ mostly easy   _____ sometimes hard and
                                                     sometimes easy

6. I work better:

_____ alone   _____ in a group   _____ both ways

7. A special talent I want to develop is: _____

_____

_____

8. My secret goal is: _____

_____

9. When I think about the future, here's what I want to be like: _____

_____

_____

10. Steps I can take to reach my goals are: _____

_____

_____

_____

What the Quizzes Tell You

For each quiz, look at your responses. Then read the following explanations to learn what your responses may mean. Keep this in mind: The quizzes are meant to help you know yourself better. Nobody is *one* way *all* of the time. Still, you can learn things about yourself and your character by looking at your responses and thinking about what they could mean.

My Character Muscles (see page 7)

Look at the right-hand column on the quiz. Did you put any checks in that column? These checks tell you the character traits you need to build.

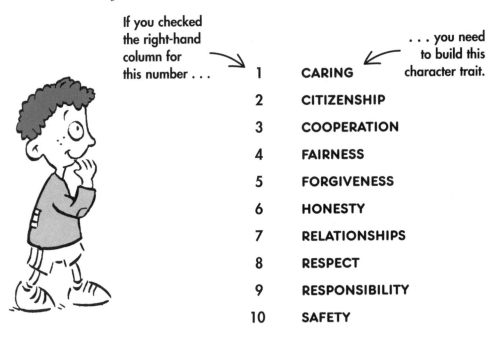

If you checked the right-hand column for this number . . .

. . . you need to build this character trait.

1	CARING
2	CITIZENSHIP
3	COOPERATION
4	FAIRNESS
5	FORGIVENESS
6	HONESTY
7	RELATIONSHIPS
8	RESPECT
9	RESPONSIBILITY
10	SAFETY

Decide which trait you want to work on first. Look it up in the contents and turn to that chapter. You'll find all kinds of ideas to help you build that trait.

My Family and Friends (see page 8)

Which column has the most checks?

If you have 11–15 "Most of the time" checks, you probably get along pretty well with your family and friends. You might enjoy reading the chapter on "Relationships" (it starts on page 90) and doing some of the activities.

If you have 6–10 "Most of the time" checks, you probably get along with your friends and family some, but not most, of the time. You'll probably find it helpful to read the chapter on "Relationships."

If you have 0–5 "Most of the time" checks, you'll want to work on the "Relationships" chapter. It can help you find ways to get along better and be happier.

What's My Personal Style? (see page 9)

For this quiz, there's no "right" answer. Still, each style means something. Knowing your style may help you choose which chapter or chapters you most want to work on.

If you checked 1, you're a person who likes to be alone. You probably work well when left to do a job by yourself. Most likely, you're pretty at ease with yourself. You may not care too much about what other people think. In other words, you're independent.

This is a good way to be. It may make a difference, though, in how you get along with people. Maybe you'll want to find some ways to work with others more easily. If that's how you feel, take a look at these chapters: "Caring" (beginning on page 17), "Cooperation" (page 41), and "Relationships" (page 90).

> **IMPORTANT!**
> Being independent isn't the same as being alone and unhappy. If you *never* want to be with other people, or if you feel lonely a lot of the time, share these feelings with a grown-up. You might talk with a parent or guardian, a teacher, the school counselor, or an adult at your place of worship. Find someone you trust and ask for help.

If you checked 2, you're probably a very friendly person, one who's happiest around other people. This is a good way to be, too. Since you seem to prefer to work with others, you might like to start with one of these chapters: "Citizenship" (beginning on page 28), "Cooperation" (page 41), "Respect" (page 107), or "Responsibility" (page 120).

If you checked 3, you're somewhere in between—a mix of independent and friendly. You like both being alone and working or playing in groups. This is a good way to be, too. You might want to begin with any chapter that interests you.

A Snapshot of Me (see pages 10–11)

There are no right or wrong answers for this page, either. Use your answers to help you choose which character traits to work on. You might want to complete "A Snapshot of Me" again in a few months, or even a few years from now. It will be interesting to see what character muscles you've built and how your goals and interests have changed.

What's Next?

You've finished the quizzes and thought about the character traits. Now it's time to start building your character muscles. Decide which trait you want to begin with, look in the contents to find it, and turn to the chapter for that trait. (If you just can't decide, go ahead and start with the first trait, "Caring.") Make a copy of the "Building My Character Muscles" chart (on page 16) and write the name of the muscle (trait) you'll be working on first. (If you want to work on more than one at a time, make extra copies of the page.) Use the chart to keep track of how you're doing day by day. Let's begin!

Sample of a completed "Building My Character Muscles" chart

Building My Character Muscles

Name _____ Jared _____

Character muscle I want to build: _____ Relationships _____   Date _____ November 7th _____

Sunday	Monday	Tuesday	Wednesday	Thursday	Friday	Saturday
Walked with Grampa	Played catch with Dad		Reading _Out of the Dust_	Played mini-golf with Mom	Invited Holly over	Went on a "Penny Ride"
	Made dinner with Joe				Helped Dad clean	
						Read to Sam

How am I doing? _____ **Need more practice**

I'll work another week on this trait. __x__ Yes   __x__ I'm improving   _____ Great!

I'll start working on a different trait. __x__ Yes   _____ No

Here's why: _____ I want to keep building more character traits. _____

Building My Character Muscles

Name _____

Date _____

Character muscle I want to build: _____

Sunday	Monday	Tuesday	Wednesday	Thursday	Friday	Saturday

How am I doing? _____ **Need more practice** _____ **I'm improving** _____ **Great!**

I'll work another week on this trait. _____ **Yes** _____ **No**

I'll start working on a different trait. _____ **Yes** _____ **No**

Here's why:

From *Being Your Best: Character Building for Kids 7–10* by Barbara A. Lewis copyright © 2000. Free Spirit Publishing Inc., Minneapolis, MN: 800/735-7323; *www.freespirit.com*. This page may be photocopied for individual, classroom, or group work only.

CARING

Taylor Meehan fixing sandwiches for the Salvation Army Community Dining Room

Someone Who Cares

Taylor Meehan and a New Pair of Shoes
Park City, Utah

Eleven-year-old Taylor Meehan and his mother serve sandwiches at the Salvation Army Community Dining Room in Salt Lake City, Utah. Once a month, they drive into the city to make and serve sandwiches to hundreds of homeless people. Many of the people have families with small children.

On a frosty night in January, the wind wailed and whirled snow through the open door of the dining room as 600 people lined up. Taylor carried trays back and forth between the kitchen and the serving table. He spoke with a man who was shivering in a thin, wet sweatshirt. The man shuffled his feet because his shoes were too small. Taylor ran to the back warehouse to hunt for extra shoes, but there weren't any. All he could find was a pair of ladies' fuzzy pink slippers.

Taylor hurried back into the dining hall. Even though the floor oozed with mud from wet boots and shoes, he knelt down next to the shivering man. Laughing, he stuck his own big feet out and pressed them against the stranger's. "Mine are the same size as yours," Taylor shouted above the noisy voices. The man smiled back from behind a thick mustache.

Gently, Taylor pulled off the man's wet shoes. The bottom of one shoe flapped loosely away from the top. Taylor placed the worn shoes on the floor. Then he took off his own new shoes and dry socks. He held one of the socks to his nose. "Whew!" he exclaimed, wiggling his nose. The man laughed.

Taylor felt the icy cold of the man's feet as he pulled the dry socks onto them. He carefully guided the man's stiff feet into the warm shoes. The man rubbed his eyes and spoke to him in Spanish. He placed his hand softly on Taylor's shoulder.

Taylor bounced up, grinning. He looked down at his own pink toes in the puddles of muddy water and laughed. He walked over to his mom. "Are you mad at me, Mom?" he asked, knowing he had just given away his new basketball shoes.

But his mom didn't look mad. She looked happy, and her eyes were wet. She shook her head and hugged Taylor so tight he thought she'd squish the stuffings out of him. "How could I be mad at such a kind thing?" she exclaimed. "But guess what, Mr. Taylor," Mom added with a chuckle. "You get to wear the fuzzy pink slippers till I can take you to a store!"

Caring—What Does It Mean?

"What's important in life is how we treat each other."
—Hana Ivanhoe, 15

One day a large mourning dove flew into a window in our home. He fell in a heap of feathers to the deck and didn't move. Suddenly, another dove swooped down to the fallen bird. The second dove began cooing and swinging her head back and forth. She stayed with the first bird for about twenty minutes, coaxing it. Then the large dove stood up on his feet. The smaller bird's voice changed to a sharp chirp that sounded like scolding. She hopped two feet away and chirped until the big dove finally ruffled his feathers and flew off with his mate. By staying and helping her mate, the second dove seemed to show that she cared about him.

Caring is about how we treat each other. Showing concern, being kind, sharing, helping, and giving are all ways that we show we care. If you share your candy bar with your little brother or help your dad clean up the kitchen, you're showing that you care. If you pick up all the scraps of paper off the floor of your classroom, you're showing your teacher that you care. You show your grandmother you care when you sit on the floor so she can have your chair. You show your neighbors you care when you take their newspaper up to their door or shovel their snow.

Every day there are hundreds of ways you can show you care. And one of the nicest things about caring for others is that they're likely to be kind to *you* in return.

"That's not so," you might say. "I let my friend borrow my bike, and she bent the fenders. She didn't even say she was sorry!"

It's true that people won't *always* treat you in the same caring way you treat them. But over time, you'll find that friends, family, and teachers will usually appreciate your kind actions and show kindness back to you.

Suppose you threw a beach ball into the ocean. The ball would return to you, no matter how hard or far you threw it. Those waves would keep rolling in, and before you knew it, your beach ball would come bobbing back to shore.

Kind words and actions are like that. You toss them out, and before you know it, someone says or does something to show that he or she cares about *you.* Caring makes the world a better place for everyone.

How Can You Show That You Care?

There are many ways you can show others that you care about them. Four important ways are through your words, actions, thoughts, and gifts.

Caring Words

You can say kind things to other people, even people you don't like very much. You might be wondering, "Why should I say something nice to someone I don't like?" Often, when we think we don't like someone, the truth is that we don't like something the person does or a certain thing about the person. Most people want to be liked. If you can think of something nice to say, maybe you'll be surprised. The person might say something kind back to *you.*

There are other ways to show caring with words. You can listen to someone who's sad and say "I know how you feel." You can see that a friend is excited and say "Wow! I'm so happy for you!" You can give someone a compliment.

Sometimes the kindest words are the ones you *don't* say. Don't talk about people behind their backs. Don't spread rumors or tell mean stories—even if you think they're true. Think about how you would feel if someone said mean things about you.

Caring Actions

You can help and you can share. You might make your sister's bed. You might help someone who's struggling with homework. When you feed your friend's gerbil while her family is on vacation, you show you care about animals and your friend. Sharing your popcorn, your toys, and your time shows that you care, too.

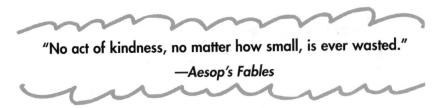

"No act of kindness, no matter how small, is ever wasted."

—Aesop's Fables

Caring Thoughts

Thinking good things about other people can help them, because they might feel the kind thoughts you send their way. And caring thoughts can lead to caring actions: What you think about is often what you do. Kind thoughts about someone else can help *you*, too. When you think good thoughts about a person, it helps you feel more happy and peaceful inside.

Try it and see. Maybe you feel a little jealous because your friend has lots of toys and games, and you don't. Don't make yourself more jealous by thinking grumpy thoughts like "That's not fair!" or "He's so lucky—how come I'm not?" Instead, think of what you like about your friend. You might think, "He's a good friend—he saves me a seat on the bus." Or, "He usually shares his games. It's nice to have such a thoughtful friend."

Caring Gifts

You can buy gifts, but often the ones you make are an even better way to show that you care. You might make a card for your cousin. Or you could give the clean, warm mittens and coat that don't fit you anymore to a shelter. Maybe you and your mom can help plant a tree in your neighbor's front yard—that would be a gift for everyone who walked or rode by. You don't have to give gifts just on birthdays or holidays. Give when you're in the mood—and when you're not. Remember, when you do something kind, it can make you feel good inside. You might be in a better mood after you give someone a gift.

6 WAYS TO GROW IN CARING

Care about others. Be kind, helpful, and sharing.

Ask about other people. Be a good listener.

Respect all people, property, animals, and the earth.

Include others. Watch to see if anyone feels lonely or left out, and include that person.

Never hold a grudge. Forgive others, and they will probably forgive you, too.

Give to others. Help other people feel good, learn, and grow.

What If?

Here are some situations for you to think about, write about, talk about, or act out.

1. Your brother never puts his toy trucks away, so you decide to do something nice for him. You start to put his trucks away every night before you go to bed. You're doing something kind for your brother, but are you really helping him? Why or why not? What is another way to show you care?

2. You have a friend who doesn't like to share her toys with you. Do you let her play with *your* toys? What might you do to help your friend and also show you care?

3. A new family has moved to your neighborhood from another country. They had to leave most of their possessions in their old home, so the kids have very few clothes. You want to show the newcomers that you care. You try to give some of your clothes to a girl in the family who's about your age. She shakes her head no and turns away from you. Why do you think she does that? How might you help this family understand that you care about them?

More Ways to Show Caring

Here are some activities you can do to show other people that you care about them.

Make Kindness Cards

Here's what you'll need:

- File cards or paper and scissors
- Pen or fine-line marker
- Shoe box
- *If you wish:* Materials for decorating the box (such as construction or wrapping paper, glue stick, markers, ribbon, and yarn)

Make kindness cards with ideas of kind things you can do for your family and friends. Write a kind act on each file card. (If you use paper, cut the paper into strips to write on.) Write as many kind acts as you can think of. Put the cards in a box. Decorate and label the box if you want to. Every morning, take a kindness card from the box. During the day, try to do that kind act at least once. Keep adding new cards to the box when you think of other kind acts to do.

Here are some ideas for kind acts. You can think of more.

At home:

- Empty the wastebasket.
- Read to your younger sister.
- Let someone else choose a TV show.
- Help your grandpa shine his shoes.
- Tell your brother you love him.

At school:

- Smile at someone you don't know.
- Sit with someone you don't like very well and try to get to know the person better.
- Say "Good job!" to someone who throws, catches, or runs well.
- Share your pencil or paper.
- Offer to straighten the books on the bookshelf.

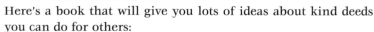

FIND OUT MORE . . .

Here's a book that will give you lots of ideas about kind deeds you can do for others:

Kids' Random Acts of Kindness by the editors of Conari Press (Emeryville, CA: Conari Press, 1994). Kids from around the world tell their own stories of kind acts.

Plan and Do a Service

A kind act that we do for someone else is called a **service.** You can do a service for someone in your neighborhood or school. Think of a person you might like to do something nice for. It could be a good friend or a person you don't know very well. You might collect used clothes from your friends and donate them to a family shelter. Maybe you have a neighbor who'd like a regular visitor. Decide who you'd like to do something kind for. Check with your dad or mom to be sure it's okay. Then do it!

> **IMPORTANT!**
> Always ask your mom or dad first before you do a service for someone. At school, always ask your teacher.

Write a Poem About Caring

Here's one poem about caring:

Caring means saying nice things to others:
My mother, my father, my sisters, my brothers,
My neighbors, my teachers, my friends near and far.
Caring shows people how special they are.

Write your own poem about caring. You might start with a certain word, like *caring, kind, helping, giving,* or *sharing.* Write your poem any way you'd like—it doesn't have to rhyme. If you want a little help getting started, you can begin your poem with one of these lines:

I find when I'm kind . . .
To share shows I care . . .
Caring means . . .
Caring shows others . . .
When I show that I care . . .
When I help others . . .
I like to give gifts . . .

Caring means sharing
miles and miles
of
SMILES!!!

You might want to hang your poem over your bed or give it to someone you care about. You could even turn it into a song.

Care for the Environment

The **environment** is the world around you. It's the home you live in, the streets you walk on, and the classrooms and halls in your school. It's the air you breathe, the lakes or rivers you swim in, the trees you climb, and the prairie or desert you like to explore.

Talk to your family and friends about ways you can care for the environment. Together, you can do a lot to help keep the world clean and safe for everyone. Here are some things you can do:

- Collect cans, bottles, and plastic containers for recycling.
- Make gift wrap out of old newspapers.
- Pick up litter along a highway or clean up an empty lot. (Be sure to do these activities with an adult.)
- Plant a garden or a tree.
- Find a home for an animal that needs one.

REMINDER:
Don't forget to keep track of your progress on the "Building My Character Muscles" chart (page 16).

Read Stories About Caring

Charlotte's Web by E.B. White (New York: Harper & Row, 1952). A spider cares for a pig and saves his life. Ages 7–11.

The Life and Times of Mother Teresa by Tanya Rice (Broomall, PA: Chelsea House, 1998). Read about this caring Catholic nun who received the Nobel Prize for her work with sick and poor people in India and other places in the world. Ages 9–12.

The Music of Dolphins by Karen Hesse (New York: Scholastic, 1996). Mila is rescued off the coast of Florida after having been raised by dolphins. The more she learns of unkindness among human beings, the more she longs for her ocean home among the dolphins. Ages 7–11.

Out of Darkness: The Story of Louis Braille by Russell Freedman (New York: Clarion Books, 1997). A biography of nineteenth-century Frenchman Louis Braille. When he was three years old, Braille lost his sight. He went on to develop a system of raised dots on paper (the Braille System) that makes it possible for people who are blind to read and write. Ages 8–12.

CITIZENSHIP

Aubyn C. Burnside surrounded by piles of donated suitcases

Someone Who's a Good Citizen

Aubyn C. Burnside and Suitcases for Kids
Hickory, North Carolina

Foster children are kids who can't live with the parents they were born or adopted to. Instead, they live in families where **foster parents** take care of them.

In 1996, when Aubyn Burnside was eleven years old, she decided that **foster children** needed her help. Her older sister Leslie worked with some foster kids. Leslie told Aubyn that many foster children have to move from one family to another. Aubyn felt sad when she thought about the kids who kept having to move. She thought the kids were being blown around like tumbleweeds. Leslie told her that some kids move as many as seven times while they're in foster care.

"Foster kids don't usually have suitcases," Aubyn's sister told her. "They have to grab anything they can find to pack their things in. Usually it's a garbage sack, or even a paper bag."

"Did you know that lots of foster kids carry their stuff around in garbage bags?" Aubyn asked her mother. "I'd hate that! I'd feel like *I* was garbage."

Aubyn went to work. She wrote a flyer asking people to **donate** suitcases for foster kids. She called her project Suitcases for Kids. She printed 1,000 flyers and took them to churches, malls, grocery stores, and museums.

Donate means to give something to an organization.

Then Aubyn walked through the door to her front porch. She plopped down on the steps and waited for suitcases. She watched the crab apple trees drop their fruit, but no one brought a suitcase.

Tired of waiting, Aubyn asked her mom if she could use her savings of $50 to buy some suitcases. Her mom said yes. Aubyn's family donated some money, too.

Not long after that, suitcases started arriving at Aubyn's door. People dropped them off all day and into the evening. Aubyn piled the suitcases in the living room.

A friend pointed to the ceiling-high pile of suitcases. "You look like you *live* in a suitcase," she laughed.

Aubyn asked her brother Welland to be junior chairman of Suitcases for Kids. She asked some other friends to help, too. Aubyn and her friends borrowed their parents' cars (and their parents) and took 170 suitcases to the Catawba County Department of Social Services. There, officials agreed to give their support to Aubyn's project.

Still more suitcases poured in. Before she knew it, Aubyn was telling about her idea at the North Carolina Foster Care Directors meeting. She made a twelve-page starter kit to show other people how do a project like hers. She traveled to other states to teach people how to set up Suitcases for Kids.

Then Oprah Winfrey asked Aubyn to be on her show. After that, the idea of Suitcases for Kids spread like flower seeds in the wind. Soon Aubyn received many awards, and more people and businesses began to help pay for her program.

Aubyn also gave her Christmas and birthday money to foster kids. The money would help high-school kids buy yearbooks and class rings, rent tuxedos for proms, and pay graduation fees.

Before long, Aubyn had started branches of Suitcases for Kids in forty-nine states and Canada. "It makes me feel really good, because these kids truly need help," Aubyn told her sister.

A fourteen-year-old boy in Burke County, North Carolina, picked out a suitcase and told Aubyn, "That's the best gift I've ever gotten."

Aubyn looked at the sparkle in the boy's eyes. "Me, too," she grinned.

FIND OUT MORE . . .

If you'd like to start a Suitcases for Kids chapter in your area or donate used luggage, write to:

Suitcases for Kids
P.O. Box 669
Newton, NC 28658

Citizenship—
What Does It Mean?

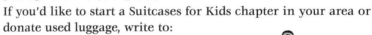

"The future depends entirely on what each of us does every day."
—Gloria Steinem

First through eighth graders at Trahagen School in Mount Vernon, New York, practice good citizenship by showing respect for other people and the earth. They work together to recycle, garden, plant trees, and write a newsletter.

Jason Dean Crowe of Newburgh, Indiana, writes and edits his own newspaper, *The Informer.* He publishes six issues a year. Jason is twelve years old and works for world peace. He donates money his paper earns to the American Cancer Society because his grandmother died of cancer. His paper goes to people in more than twenty-five states and twelve countries.

Both Jason and the kids at Trahagen School understand something important: Part of living in a **democracy** is to be a good **citizen.**

A democracy is a form of government. In a democracy, people choose their leaders by voting. The people and the leaders decide what laws everyone will follow. In a democracy, people have certain freedoms. They have the right to vote. They usually have the right to meet in groups and to choose their own religion. That *doesn't* mean people have the freedom to do anything they want. For example, one person doesn't have the right to harm or hurt someone else.

All countries have rules or laws that people must follow. Think about some of the laws in your own country. You know it's against the law to steal. You know you don't have the right to beat anybody up. But if you live in a democracy, you *do* have many freedoms. You're free to speak out about what you believe. Together with your family, you can choose where to live, what to read or watch on TV, and who to spend your time with. When you're older, you'll be free to choose what job you want. When you're an adult, you'll have the right to vote.

In the meantime, you can choose whether you want to eat chocolate or pistachio ice cream. You can decide if you want to read a book about angleworms or chimpanzees. And if you're a good citizen, you recycle your plastic ice-cream dish or put the empty wrapper in the trash can. You return the book to the library on or before the day it's due.

Following the rules and laws in your home or community is one way you show good **citizenship.** A citizen is a person who lives in a community. In a democracy, a citizen has both rights and responsibilities. As a good citizen, you do two important things:

- You use your freedom (rights) wisely.
- You do things to help at home and school and in your neighborhood and community (responsibilities).

If you're a good citizen, people will admire you. Parents, teachers, and other adults will trust you more and will more likely want you to be part of activities.

As a good citizen, you're a sort of "take charge of yourself" kid. You know the rules and you follow them. No one else has to tell you to do that. You look for ways to help your home and school be nice places for everyone. Other people will see this and look at you as a leader. When you grow up, you might be a leader in your town or even your country, because you will already have practiced being a good citizen.

How Can You Be a Good Citizen?

There are lots of ways to show that you're a good citizen. Three important ways are to show respect, be involved, and serve others.

Show Respect

You're a good citizen when you care about the people, animals, places, and things around you. You show that you care by treating them all with respect. One way to show respect is by obeying all the rules and laws in your community, your home, and your school. That means you don't dig a hole in your school desk with your pencil or write **graffiti** (pictures, names, or words) on walls and doors. It means that you *do* water plants, feed the cat, and speak kindly to your parents, teachers, friends, sisters, and brothers.

In a democracy, being a good citizen can also mean that you're **patriotic**—that you love your country. You can show this when you salute the flag and treat it with respect. You can also show it when you sing patriotic songs such as "The Star-Spangled Banner" or "O Canada." As a patriotic citizen, you do what you can to learn about your nation's laws and customs.

Be Involved

There are lots of ways to be involved. One way is to work with your classmates and teachers to make rules about how people at school can get along together. Another way is to encourage your dad and mom and other adults to vote. Offer to go with them to the polling (voting) place.

And you don't have to be old enough to vote before you can have a say in your government. With your family, class, or group, you can visit a town or county council meeting to see how laws are made and changed. You might even sign up to talk to the council about something important that needs fixing. Maybe you know a street that needs a stop sign or a playground where the steps on the slide are broken.

If you care about a law, you can **lobby** for or against it. That means you can go to your city council, state house, or state capitol and tell the lawmakers how you want them to vote. Or you can write letters to your lawmakers. Maybe you want a law that lowers the speed limit in neighborhoods where kids play. Maybe you want your government to spend money on a new library or sports stadium. Maybe you want it *not* to spend money on those things. You can think of something on your own. Get a trusted adult to help you with this.

If you're a good citizen, you watch out for other people, animals, trees, and **property** (things that belong to people). When you see something happen that's unfair or unsafe, say something! Speaking up is an important way to be involved. Tell your mom, dad, teacher, club leader, coach, or another adult you trust.

Serve

Serve in your community, your school, and your home. What can you do? Fix things up. Plant bushes. Rake leaves. Recycle batteries. Remember to walk—not run—in the halls at school. Take a few minutes to clean out the dust bunnies from under your bed. These are simple ways, but they all show that you can be a good citizen.

FIND OUT MORE . . .

Here's a book that has lots of ideas for taking action to be a good citizen:

The Kid's Guide to Social Action: How to Solve the Social Problems You Choose—and Turn Creative Thinking into Positive Action (Revised, Expanded, Updated Edition) by Barbara A. Lewis (Minneapolis: Free Spirit Publishing, 1998). Step-by-step instructions show how to write letters, do interviews, make speeches, raise money, and more. Ages 10 and up.

7 WAYS TO BE A GOOD CITIZEN

Care about your community, state or province, and country. Obey the laws and rules.

Improve something in your home or neighborhood.

Take the time to learn about how your government works.

Involve yourself by becoming a leader at school or at your place of worship.

Zero in on something that needs fixing and work with others to do the job.

Encourage your parents and other adults you know to vote.

Never forget to show respect for people, animals, plants, and property.

What If?

Here are some situations for you to think about, write about, talk about, or act out.

1. Your best friend has a dog named Bailey. You really love Bailey. You know that your friend is in charge of feeding him and giving him fresh water. But you also see that your friend doesn't always take good care of Bailey. Sometimes the food in the dog dish is crusty. Sometimes the water dish is empty. If you're a good citizen, do you have a responsibility to do anything? If so, what? If not, why?

2. There's a girl in your class who told you secretly that her father hits her and hurts her. She showed you bruises on her back, but asked you never to tell anyone. If you're a good citizen, should you keep your friend's secret? If so, why? If not, what should you do about it?

> **IMPORTANT!**
> If you are being hurt by someone, you can get help. Talk to an adult you trust. That might be your dad or mom. Or it might be a teacher, an aunt or uncle, a counselor at school, or someone at your place of worship.

3. Your mom isn't home. While the sitter's busy putting your two-year-old brother to bed, you start playing hockey in the kitchen with the new hockey stick you got for your birthday. You know the rule: You're never supposed to use the hockey stick indoors. But it's raining outside. While you play, you accidentally hit the cupboard with the stick. It dents the door and scrapes off some paint. Now you don't know what to do. You could tell your mom, but if you do she'll probably take away your hockey stick. You could say nothing and hope she doesn't notice. And there's a little voice inside you that says you could blame it on your younger brother. No matter what, you've decided that you *won't* break the rule again. But should you tell the truth about what happened? As a good citizen, what should you do? What do you think will happen as a result?

4. You and your family just learned that the after-school program you go to may soon close. The director sent a letter that says there's not enough money to keep it going. You know that you're not the only kid whose parents aren't home when school gets out. You and your classmates need a safe place to play and learn after school. As good citizens, what can you and your family do?

More Ways to Be a Good Citizen

Here are some activities you can do to get in the habit of good citizenship.

Learn About Good Citizens

Ask a librarian or bookstore clerk to help you find a book or video about an important citizen in history or today. There are lots of people you could read about. Here are just a few ideas: Abigail Adams, Marie Curie, Frederick Douglass, Thomas Edison, Benjamin Franklin, Indira Gandhi, Thomas Jefferson, Chief Joseph, Martin Luther King Jr., Daw Aung San Suu Kyi, Rosa Parks, Oscar Arias Sánchez, Mother Teresa, Harriet Tubman, and Elie Wiesel. Learn what you can about why the person you choose was or is a good citizen. Did the person do something to help a community, a country, or the world?

Have Family Meetings

Family meetings are a great way to make plans and solve problems together. You can think about them as democracy at home. If you have a family meeting each week, everyone will know they'll have a chance to talk over important things. To get your family started, decide together when and where to meet. For example, you might meet every Thursday night right after supper. Or you might meet first thing every Saturday morning.

Run your meetings like a democracy. Take turns being **chairperson** (the person in charge of the meeting) and **recorder** (the person who writes down important things you talk about). If you have a problem to talk about, let each person explain his or her feelings and ideas about it. Listen respectfully. Vote on a way to try to solve the problem. If you want to plan something fun like a cookout or a trip to the zoo, have everyone offer suggestions. Talk about the ideas and choose the one most people agree to.

The family meeting will let everyone practice working together as a democracy. You'll share ideas, show respect, and make decisions by voting. Of course, your parents or guardians are still in charge of the family. They'll probably have some rules that they won't put up for a vote. But you'll find there are lots of decisions you and your family will be able to make together.

A FAMILY MEETING PLAN

Here's one plan you could follow at each family meeting:

1. Read the notes the recorder took at the last meeting.
2. Talk about old business (problems or plans you discussed at the last meeting).
3. Talk about new business (new things you want to plan or talk about).
4. Finish the meeting with a fun activity like a story or game.

> "To define democracy in one word,
> we must use the word 'cooperation.'"
> —Dwight D. Eisenhower, 34th U.S. president

Go with Your Parents to Vote

The next time there's an election, go with your dad or mom to vote. Encourage your neighbors, teachers, and other adults to vote, too. To find out what you need to know about the election, call or have an adult call the voter registration office or the League of Women Voters. (You can find local phone numbers in your telephone book.) Have these questions ready:

- When will the election be?
- Where will it be held?
- How do people register (sign up) to vote?
- Where can I learn about the people and subjects to vote about?

REMINDER: Don't forget to keep track of your progress on the "Building My Character Muscles" chart (page 16).

FIND OUT MORE . . .

Here's a chance for *you* to vote. This organization makes it possible for young people to visit polling (voting) places on election days. Kids get to vote on the same issues and candidates that adults are voting for. Write to the organization, or ask your dad or mom if you may call. If there's a computer you can use, visit the Web site.

Kids Voting USA
398 South Mill Avenue, Suite 304
Tempe, AZ 85281
Phone number: (480) 921-3727
Web site: *www.kidsvotingusa.org*

Read Stories About Citizenship

Brother Eagle, Sister Sky: A Message from Chief Seattle by Susan Jeffers (New York: Dial Books for Young Readers, 1991). A story based on a speech made by Chief Seattle 150 years ago about protecting the environment. Ages 4–8.

I, Juan De Pareja by Elizabeth Borton De Trevino (New York: Farrar, Straus & Giroux, 1995). Based on the true story of a slave who was given to the great Spanish painter Velazquez. The relationship between the two men became one of friendship and equality. Ages 4–8.

Molly's Pilgrim by Barbara Cohen (New York: Yearling Books, 1990). Molly's family has moved to America from Russia. Her classmates make fun of her accent, her clothes, and her doll, which her mother has dressed in Russian clothes. The teacher helps them see that Molly's mother is a modern Pilgrim who came to America for religious freedom. Ages 6–9.

The Streets Are Free by Kurusa (Buffalo, NY: Firefly Books, 1995). A group of children lose their play area that had trees and streams. They begin to play in the streets. The neighborhood works together to make a playground for the children. Ages 8–10.

Thunder Cave by Roland Smith (New York: Hyperion, 1997). Young Jacob Lansa travels to Kenya in search of his father. In Kenya, Jacob faces many life-threatening challenges as he tries to save a herd of elephants from dry weather and hunters. Ages 8–11.

COOPERATION

Kanesha Sonee Johnson

Someone Who Cooperates

Kanesha Sonee Johnson Brings Classmates Together
Hawthorne, California

Kanesha Sonee Johnson started fifth grade at Williams Elementary School in Hawthorne, California. She was placed in a **bilingual** class. Kanesha saw that the Vietnamese and African-American kids kept to themselves. They didn't work together in the classroom unless the teacher told them to. At recess, when kids played four-square or volleyball, Vietnamese kids chose other Vietnamese kids to be on their teams. African-American kids chose other African-Americans.

Although Kanesha was African-American, she wanted to make friends with the Vietnamese kids. She thought about it and came up with an idea. She was a very good student who always got A's in language and reading, so she offered to teach English to Thein, Van, and Thonh. The three children agreed. Kanesha gave them homework sentences to

Bilingual means using two different languages, like English and Vietnamese. A bilingual class is one where some of the kids speak English and some speak a different language.

41

write in English. She told them to learn how to pronounce all the words. Before class in the mornings, the three kids handed their homework to Kanesha. She corrected their papers and helped them with mistakes. Thein, Van, and Thonh began to learn English faster.

But Kanesha's African-American friends started to call her names. They teased her because she was smart and because she was trying to help kids learn English.

"They don't understand," Kanesha thought. She told the friends who teased her, "If we all play together and cooperate, we'll have more fun."

After school one day, Kanesha told her troubles to her mother. "They make fun of me," Kanesha said. "Now the only kids I can play with are Thein, Van, and Thonh. Even my old friends are saying 'You think you're so smart!' And they talk about me behind my back."

Kanesha's mother smiled and cupped her daughter's chin in her hand. "Honey," she said, "just ignore it. When they're talking about you, that means you're on their minds." Kanesha knew what her mother meant. If she was on the kids' minds, they must be thinking about what she said about cooperating.

So Kanesha kept helping Thein, Van, and Thonh learn English. And she continued telling her other friends that they should play with the Vietnamese kids, too. Soon some of Kanesha's friends invited her and her three Vietnamese classmates to play volleyball with them. Before you could count backward from ten in Vietnamese, the two groups were playing together in mixed teams. The name-calling stopped.

When Thonh learned he had to move away, he told the fifth-grade teacher, Mr. Tran, "I'm going to miss Kanesha's homework. It was helping me a lot. I have more friends now, too." That was the first time Mr. Tran learned that Kanesha had been teaching the kids English. He smiled at her and thanked her for the help.

"It's okay," Kanesha grinned. "If we all learn to cooperate, then our lives will be smoother and more peaceful. There's a lot we can learn from each other."

Cooperation— What Does It Mean?

"Working together is like making a word.
If one of the letters is missing, the word just won't make sense."

—Hien Le, 11

Did you ever think about how all the parts of your body work together to help you to live? If your brain, nerves, and muscles didn't work together, you wouldn't be able to skip, lick an ice-cream cone, or even sleep.

People need to work together, too. If musicians in a band didn't do that, how would their music sound? If ball players didn't work with their coach and each other, how could they play the game as a team? People need to **cooperate** in order to get along and get things done.

Cooperation means working or playing together peacefully. When you cooperate with other people, you all make an effort to do something together. Cooperating lets you accomplish things that you can't do alone. It also lets you get along better with your parents, friends, brothers, and sisters. "No way!" you might say. "I can't cooperate with my sister. We always fight because she teases me." It's true that you can't *make* your sister, or anybody else, do what you want her to do. But you can choose how *you'll* act and what *you'll* do.

People get angry. They don't always agree with each other. It's normal and natural for human beings to have disagreements. Disagreeing isn't the problem. The problem is in *how* you work out the disagreement. Will you be angry and hit someone? Or will you talk about your problem with your sister or friend and then choose something to do that both of you can agree on?

"Why should I do that?" you might wonder. Because if you learn to cooperate better, you'll feel better about yourself. You'll probably have more friends and fight and argue with them less often. Your parents and teachers will probably respect you more, too. Learning to cooperate can help you get along with people and be a happier person.

How Can You Cooperate?

Working together to reach a goal is one way that people cooperate. Another way is by making an effort to solve problems peacefully—without yelling, hitting, or saying mean things. These things might not be easy to do at first. But lots of things don't start out easy.

Think about learning to ride a bike. That takes time and practice. You might wobble and fall off the bike many times before you learn how to make smooth turns and "pop wheelies." The same is true for learning to cooperate with people. It takes practice, too.

When people disagree and start to fight about a problem, they have a **conflict.** There are two words that can help you remember ways to cooperate and solve conflicts peacefully: TALKS and CALM.

"I always tumble into trouble when I lose my temper."

—*Jane Louise Curry*

Use TALKS to Solve a Problem

When you want to work out a problem with someone, it helps to have a plan. Here's a cooperation
plan with words to help you remember the steps to
follow. It's called TALKS, which stands for the first
word of each step: Talk, Act, Listen, Keep, and Share.

TALKS—5 STEPS FOR TALKING ABOUT A PROBLEM

Talk about what happened. Be honest. Explain why
each of you did what you did. Were you tired? Angry?
Grumpy?

Act and talk politely. Talk about the *problem,* not the
person. Don't say something like "I hate you for
taking my pencil." Instead, say, "I don't like it when
someone takes my pencil." Or, "I don't like it when
my toys are missing."

Listen to the other person's side of the story. Think
about how he or she might feel. Ask questions so you
understand. Learning to listen takes lots of practice.
Don't give up!

Keep trying to cooperate. Have an open mind. If one
idea doesn't work, try another.

Share in finding a solution. Find an answer to your
problem that both of you can agree on.

IMPORTANT!

If someone won't stop teasing or fighting, it's time to ask a
grown-up for help. Ask your teacher, dad, mom, or another adult
to help the two of you talk together and solve the problem.

Here's an example of two kids using TALKS to solve a problem. See if you can tell how they followed each step:

T   **Anika:** "My pencil's gone. Do you know where it is? You have one just like it. Is that my pencil you have?"

     Jamal: "No, this is mine. I didn't take yours."

A   **Anika:** "I'm *so* mad I lost that pencil. It was my favorite one!"

L   **Jamal:** "But I didn't take it. *I* feel bad if you think I did."

K   **Anika:** "It's gone, so somebody must have taken it. Your pencil's just like mine—how do you know that one's yours?"

     Jamal: "I promise I didn't take it. Don't you believe me?"

     Anika: "I guess I do."

S   **Jamal:** "Let's look together. Maybe it rolled under the cupboard. I'll check there."

     Anika: "And I'll look through my desk again."

     Jamal: "And we can ask if anybody else has seen it. If we don't find it, we can take turns using mine. I've got other pencils I can use."

     Anika: "Thanks."

Here's something to think about: It's easier to pull weeds from a garden when they're tiny. The same is true about problems with other people. It's easier to avoid fighting by talking things over before they get worse.

When You're Angry, Work to Be CALM

Do you get into lots of fights? Do other kids pick fights with you? Are you often mad at someone? Do some kids act like they're afraid of you? If you said yes to any of these questions, you might need to learn how to handle your anger.

We all get angry sometimes. That's okay. But it's not okay to hit, yell, fight, or name-call when we're mad about something. There are lots of ways to let angry feelings out and to deal with problems that upset you. To do this, you can learn steps for being CALM. CALM stands for the first word of each step: Calm, Admit, Learn, and Make.

CALM DOWN—
4 STEPS TO EASING ANGRY FEELINGS

Calm yourself down. There are lots of ways to do this. You might take a deep breath, speak slowly, or soften your voice. Or you might take time out to do something else, rest, read, or jump up and down until you're tired. Try different things to see what works for you.

Admit that you have a problem. Look at what happened and what you said or did. "I yelled." "I said something mean." "I broke the light." Don't run away or ignore it. It's okay to make mistakes if you learn from them.

Learn to share your feelings with someone. Talk about angry or upset feelings with an adult you trust. You might talk to your mom or dad, your teacher, your club leader, or someone at your place of worship. Keep looking until you find someone who will listen and talk to you about how you feel. Have the person help you find ways to deal with angry feelings.

Make a change in how you deal with anger. Decide on something safe and healthy to do when you feel angry. It's not safe or healthy to throw things, holler at people, or hit or kick someone. What can you do instead? You could try jumping jacks. You could make funny faces at yourself in the mirror. You might want to write in a journal. Decide that next time you're angry and having a conflict, you'll count to ten backwards before you speak, think of something nice to say, or walk away until you feel better.

Practice ways to handle anger. Keep practicing. Make a list of all the times you changed your angry feelings or got rid of them in a safe and peaceful way. The list will help you see how you're improving. Are you starting to get mad less often? If so, pat yourself on the back (if you can reach it).

FIND OUT MORE . . .

KidsHealth.org for Kids is a Web site you can visit to learn lots about being healthy, including ways to deal with anger. To check out these tips, go to *www.kidshealth.org/kid/* and click on "Dealing With Feelings." (You'll find other good information about health and safety at this Web site, too. Ask your mom or dad to visit the site with you.)

Another way to make a change is to talk about the conflict. When you do, show respect for the other person. If your friend teases you and you don't like it, tell the friend how you feel. Don't yell, "You make me so mad when you tease me!" Instead, use a calm voice and say, "I don't like to be teased. I wish you'd stop." Maybe you and your brother each want to play a different game. You might say to him, "How about if we play one game of each?" Or, "Why don't we draw straws?" Or, "Let's play the game you like this time, and the one I like next time."

"Peace can be made in the neighborhoods, the living rooms, the playing fields, and the classrooms of our country."

—Jimmy Carter, 39th U.S. president

Conflicts aren't good or bad—they just *are*. You can't avoid some conflicts. What's important is how you handle conflicts that occur. TALKS and CALM are two tools you can use to help you solve conflicts when they happen.

What If?

Here are some situations for you to think about, write about, talk about, or act out.

1. Your teacher has just divided your class into groups and told you that each group will be doing a service project. You're supposed to work with the other people in your group to make a plan. How will you come up with a good idea? How will you plan your project? What will you do first? Second? Third? What will you do if people disagree?

2. The kid who lives next door picks on you all the time. He calls you names and takes your toys. How might you stand up for yourself and still show respect (be nice)? What can you do to help your neighbor understand how you feel? What could you do to help both of you cooperate better?

3. You like to tell other people when they're doing something wrong. But your friends don't like it when you correct them. They think you're being bossy. How can you encourage friends to do what's right without being bossy?

4. You and your sister want to go to the park to play. Your grandma has told you both to clean your room before you go. How can you cooperate and finish quickly so you can get to the park?

More Ways to Cooperate

Here are some activities that will help you cooperate.

Make a Cooperation Collage

Here's what you'll need:

- Paper or posterboard
- Scissors
- Glue stick
- Magazines for cutting out pictures
  (ask permission before you cut!)
- Colored pencils or markers

A **collage** is a poster with lots of different pictures on it. There are many ways you could make a collage about cooperation. You could show pictures of people sharing, taking turns, working together, and treating each other with respect. Or you could show pictures of people *not* cooperating and write a sentence under each saying what the people can do to get along better. You could cut out words instead of pictures, choosing words about cooperation ("Share," "Take turns," "Talk it over," "Work together," "Stay calm"). You can think of other ideas.

Show your collage to your family and friends. Talk with them about cooperation and what it means. Tape your picture on the refrigerator or pin it on a bulletin board in your room. Keep it there as a reminder to find positive ways to work with other people and peaceful ways to solve problems.

Teach Your Family About TALKS

Here's what you'll need:

- Posterboard
- Marker

Show other people in your family "TALKS—5 Steps for Talking About a Problem" (page 45). Suggest that people in your family use the steps when there's a problem or conflict. (This would be a good thing to talk about in a family meeting. See "Have Family Meetings," pages 37–38.) Make a large TALKS poster to display somewhere in your home. That way, people will be able to see it when they need to solve a problem peacefully.

Make a Cooperative Chores Chart

Here's what you'll need:
- Chart paper (such as newsprint)
- Marker or pen

Chores at home often go better when people cooperate to get them done. Talk about chores that two or more people could do together. Make a "Cooperative Chores Chart" and have people sign up to do chores together. (This is another good activity for a family meeting.) Here are some jobs that might be on your chart:

Chore	Who will do it together?
Wash and dry the dishes. ⟶	Monday, Wednesday, Friday—Grandpa and Emilio
	Tuesday, Thursday, Saturday—Marta and Gina
	Sunday—Mom and Grandpa
Dust and vacuum. ⟶	Ray and Marta
Rake and bag leaves this weekend. ⟶	Everybody!
Fold and put away laundry. ⟶	Emilio and Dad
Shop for groceries this weekend. ⟶	Dad, Mom, and Ray
Take out recycling. ⟶	Gina and Grandpa

REMINDER:
Don't forget to
keep track of
your progress
on the "Building
My Character
Muscles" chart
(page 16).

Make a Cooperation Log

Here's what you'll need:

- Notebook and pen or pencil
- *If you wish:* Materials for decorating your notebook (such as paints, markers, colored pencils, pictures cut from magazines, glue stick, ribbon, and stickers)

A **log** is a kind of list, diary, or journal. When you write in it, you tell the date and describe something that happened. (*Example:* Oct. 10—I didn't slam my door when the baby cried. Good for me! And I helped Dad set the table without being asked.) Make a "Cooperation Log" to keep track of times when you work well with others, solve problems peacefully, and handle anger in a safe, healthy way. You could use a special notebook for this. If you like, decorate your notebook.

Read Stories About Cooperation

Carrots and Miggle by Ardath Mayhar (New York: Atheneum, 1986). Carrots, a young Texas farm girl, is happy until a cousin from London comes to live in her home. Cousin Emiglia (Miggle) didn't know people could work so hard or get so dirty. It takes time for Carrots and Miggle to learn to cooperate. Ages 10–12.

Crash by Jerry Spinelli (New York: Alfred A. Knopf, 1996). When John "Crash" Coogan carries a prank too far, he learns a lesson about cooperation and caring. Ages 9–12.

Patchwork Quilt by Valerie Flournoy (New York: Dial Press, 1985). A girl helps her grandmother make a quilt that tells the story of her family and how they cooperate. Ages 5–8.

Peace Begins with You by Katherine Scholes (San Francisco, CA: Sierra Club Books/Little, Brown & Co., 1989). Shows ways to resolve conflicts at home and around the globe. Ages 6–10.

FAIRNESS

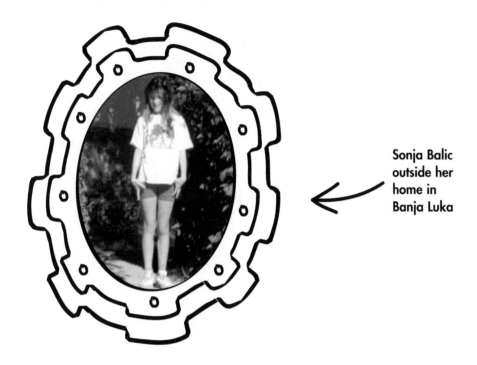

Sonja Balic outside her home in Banja Luka

Someone Who's Fair

Sonja Balic Leaves Her Bosnian Home
Banja Luka, Bosnia-Herzegovina

Sonja Balic was six years old when war began in Bosnia. She heard of children whose parents were taken away. She heard of shootings and bombings. Still, the war seemed far away from her family and home in Banja Luka, Bosnia-Herzegovina.

But not for long. The war was being fought among Serbs, Muslims, and Croats. Sonja's mother was Serbian and her dad was Muslim. Just after the war began, all the Muslims were fired from their jobs. Sonja's dad lost his job at a newspaper. After that, no one would hire him. He had to do construction work without any pay. Sonja told her father, "It isn't fair." He only nodded and hugged her close to him.

Sonja's mom, a dental assistant, wasn't fired. But Sonja's parents were still worried. She heard them talking in low voices. Her father said, "There isn't much money. No gas. Good food is getting harder to find. It gets worse every day."

Sonja didn't think food was hard to find. She knew her grandparents would share their tomatoes and cabbages. And Sonja's family grew their own carrots and potatoes.

The war still seemed far away to Sonja as she rolled on her in-line skates with her best friend, Ivana. Sometimes Sonja and Ivana hung out in the park nearby with other friends. They swung on the swings or played on the climbing bars. Sonja could fling herself all the way around on the bars. She loved skipping past the town's beautiful old castle and the Vrbas River that flowed beside it.

But when Sonja asked for a dollhouse for her eighth birthday, her mother said, "Some other time, Sonja. There isn't enough money now. It's the war."

Sonja only nodded her head. But she thought to herself, "It still isn't fair."

Sonja began to hear more bad stories about the war. There was a boy who saw his parents shot. Another boy shot his own arm off while playing with his dad's army gun. Sonja's cousins in Sarajevo had to live in their basements because their homes were bombed out.

A mosque is a Muslim place of worship.

One by one, all the **mosques** were being bombed and destroyed. Two blocks away from Sonja's home there was a beautiful mosque. One night, the mosque was bombed. The bomb also shattered the windows in Sonja's house.

Sonja asked her mother, "Why do people have to fight? I think it's stupid. We used to all be friends."

"This is true," her mother answered. "A few people decide to fight, but then the rest of us suffer, too."

Her father shook his head.

It was growing too dangerous for Muslims in Bosnia. Just before Sonja's tenth birthday, her father flew to the United States to start a new life for his family. The war no longer seemed far away. It was knocking at her door.

When their dad left, Sonja's little brother cried and wailed, "It's not fair!"

Sonja wrapped her arms around him. "Things are *not* always fair," she said. "You have to get through tough times and just keep going." He wiped his eyes and smiled up at her. But later that night, when Sonja was alone, she cried into her pillow.

The family waited for another year and a half before Sonja, her brother, and her mom were able to leave Bosnia for the United States.

Before she left, the kids at Sonja's school threw a party for her. They gave her a necklace, a locket, pictures, and phone numbers. "Come back soon," they said. Sonja swallowed hard, because she knew she might not be back for a long time.

Sonja had to leave her friends, her grandparents and other relatives, her beautiful home, and the castle by the river. It was the hardest thing she had ever done. It didn't seem fair to her that guns and armies should tear up people's lives. So Sonja decided that no matter how unfair things were around her, she would *always* treat other people fairly. That was the best way she knew to try to make the world a better place.

Fairness—What Does It Mean?

"I know, up on top you are seeing great sights,
But down at the bottom we, too, should have some rights."

—*Dr. Seuss*

Have you ever felt something wasn't **fair**? Maybe someone pushed ahead of you in line at the movies. Maybe your friend got a brand-new bike when you didn't have a bike at all. Maybe your brother can stay up later than you. Maybe the whole class had to miss recess even though only a few kids were misbehaving. Maybe you wish you had a dad who coached soccer, like your neighbor's stepdad does. Maybe someone you love got sick or hurt.

And maybe your dad, mom, or teacher has told you, "That's just the way life is. Life isn't always fair." You may wonder, "Why not?" Or, you might think, "If that's how life is, why should *I* try to be fair?"

When you're fair, other people like, trust, and respect you more. They see you as a person who's honest and who cares about others. They can look to you to be a leader and to learn from your example. When you treat them fairly, they're more likely to start acting the same way.

Fairness means treating other people the way *you* want to be treated. It means trying to give everyone rights and chances like those you have. When you're fair, you do your best to share, take turns, and treat each person with respect. You try to make things "fair and square."

Fairness *doesn't* mean that everything is equal or the same. For example, you may wish you had a dog, like your friend does. But your friend lives in a house, and you live in an apartment, where dogs aren't allowed. You can still treat your friend fairly—and play with her dog when you visit.

Lots of things in the world aren't fair. It's not fair that people are hungry or homeless. It's not fair that people suffer in wars. It's not fair that in some parts of the world, children have to work instead of going to school. Many people are aware of these problems and are trying to change things for the better. It takes time and effort to work for fairness.

Imagine a world where no one was ever fair. What would it be like? Everyone would be selfish. No one would care about anyone else. Would you want to live in that kind of world? We all need to do our best to be fair. Every act of fairness makes the world a better place.

How Can You Be Fair?

There are many ways you can work to be fair. You can share and take turns. You can decide not to be jealous of somebody else. You can show respect for people even if they're different from you. You can find a good way to act when someone isn't fair to you.

Share and Take Turns

You can take turns at recess with the swings, the slide, or with sports equipment. You can take turns playing a computer game. You can share a bag of chips or a box of markers. You can wait in line to get on the bus or use the bathroom. Other people are waiting, too, and some of them were there before you. It's fair to let them go first.

Decide Not to Be Jealous

Sometimes other people have things you don't. You might feel **jealous** and wish you could have what they have or be like them. It can be hard not to feel jealous. But being jealous just makes you unhappy. And it can make other people feel bad, too.

At softball, maybe your friend hits the ball more often than you do. What if you said to her, "It's not fair you're so good at batting!" Your friend might feel bad about her special skill. Instead, you could say, "You sure can hit that ball! How do you do it?" Then your friend will feel good, and you'll feel better, too. She might even offer to help you practice your swing.

Remember, someone else's talent might be different from yours, but you have talents and skills, too. Part of your job is to find your own special abilities and interests and then work to develop them. If you do your best not to be jealous, you might notice someone who can help you "grow" your talent. You might also find that you can help other people do the same.

"America is . . . like a quilt . . . many pieces, many colors, many sizes, all woven and held together by a common thread."

—Jesse Jackson

Respect All People

People are different from each other in lots of ways. Some people have dark skin, some have light. Some people speak English, some speak Spanish, some Vietnamese, and some

Swahili. Some people are Christian, or Jewish, or Muslim, or Buddhist. Some people are good at reading or math. Other people aren't. Some people can jump and run with ease. Other people can't.

It's not fair to ignore or be mean to someone who's different from you. Why not be friendly to people who aren't the same as you? Then you can look for ways to learn about and enjoy each other.

FIND OUT MORE . . .

Save the Children works for children's rights around the world. The organization was started by a boy who didn't think it was fair for some kids to have to work in factories. Write, call (be sure to ask permission first), or visit the Web site to get some ideas on how you can help make the world more fair for all kids.

Save the Children
54 Wilton Road
Westport, CT 06880
1-800-728-3843
Web site: *www.savethechildren.org/*

When Someone Else Isn't Fair

When someone isn't fair to you, you might feel like crying, getting mad, yelling, or doing something mean back. None of these things will help you or the other person learn to be fair to each other. Here are some ideas to try when someone's not fair to you:

- Talk about the problem with the person. You might say, "I think everyone should have a turn. Don't you?" Or, "I think each of us should have the same number of pieces."
- Ask an adult, like your teacher or parent, for help.
- Ignore what's happened. If it doesn't bother you a lot, let it go.

- Laugh it off. This can surprise people and help them get out of a mean mood.
- Change the activity. Find something else to do together.
- Leave and go somewhere else to work or play.

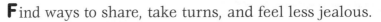

4 WAYS TO TREAT PEOPLE FAIRLY

Find ways to share, take turns, and feel less jealous.

Ask people what you can do to help make things more fair.

Include others in games and activities. Don't leave people out.

Respect people who are different from you.

What If?

Here are some situations for you to think about, write about, talk about, or act out.

1. Your brother Alex wants to take ballet lessons. Your other brother and a friend tell Alex that dancing is "sissy stuff." Is that fair? Why or why not? What might happen to Alex if he takes ballet lessons anyway? What might happen if he doesn't? What would you do or say in this situation?

2. Your mom promises to take you and your friend to an amusement park for your birthday. You can't wait to go on the roller coaster and all kinds of other fun rides. But on your birthday, you wake up and see dark clouds in the sky. It looks like it's going to be a rainy day. Your mom says, "I think we should save the amusement park for another day. It won't be fun if it rains." You cry, "That's not faaaaiiir! You promised!" Is your mom being unfair? Why or why not? Is there something you and your mom could do to help make things fair for everybody? What?

3. Your neighborhood has mostly black people and white people, and you get along fine. A new kid named Kuri moves in. Kuri's Japanese. You notice that some of your friends ignore Kuri or make fun of her. You want to help, but you're afraid they may make fun of you, too. How might you help make things more fair for Kuri *and* your friends? What might happen if you do that?

More Ways to Be Fair

Here are some activities you can do to find more ways to be fair.

Make a Fairness Pocket Card

Here's what you'll need:

- File card
- Fine-line marker (or markers in a variety of colors, if you wish)

Talk it over.
Do something else.
Talk to the teacher.

On the file card, write a list of things you can do when someone isn't fair. You might use the ideas on pages 59–60 or write other ideas in your own words. Make the card colorful if you want.

Keep your card in your pocket, backpack, or desk. When someone's not being fair with you, take a "time out" for yourself and look at your "Fairness Pocket Card." Find an idea that might help.

Make Family Chores Fair

Talk with your family about the different chores that need to be done at home. Discuss how to make chores fair for everyone. For example, is it easier to collect trash and recycle than to vacuum and dust? Or maybe one night a person has to do piles of dishes after a big meal. The next night, somebody else has to clean up after a meal of take-out pizza. Is that fair? How could you make it fair? Listen to everyone's ideas on how to make the chores fair. Try to plan a week's worth of chores in a way that feels fair to everybody. Was it hard or easy to do this? Why?

This is a good thing to do at a family meeting. See "Have Family Meetings," pages 37–38, to learn about family meetings. You might also do the same kind of activity at school to make classroom chores fair.

Start a Fairness Jar

Here's what you'll need:

- Large, clean jar, coffee can, or box with lid
- Label
- Marker
- Paper
- Scissors

Label your container, and place it where everyone in the family or class can reach it. Cut paper into slips and place the slips beside the jar. When something unfair happens to somebody, the person can write a note about what happened and place it in the jar. Once a week, meet together and talk about ways to make things more fair. (At home, this is a good thing to do at a family meeting, too.)

Make Games More Fair

Think of games you like to play with your friends—people whose skills and abilities are about the same as yours. What if you want to play the same games with younger kids, or kids with disabilities, or elderly people? How might you change the games to make them more fair for people of *unequal* ability?

Here are a few ideas for making games more fair. You can think of others:

REMINDER:
Don't forget to keep track of your progress on the "Building My Character Muscles" chart (page 16).

- **Checkers or chess.** Instead of trying to beat each other, cooperate to make the best moves for the best overall game. For every move, talk over different ways it could be played. Agree on the best one.
- **Sorry!** Send the weaker player's piece back ten spaces instead of all the way home. Or switch sides halfway through.
- **Solitaire.** Play with two people and switch turns playing the cards. If the game "comes out," you both win.

Read Stories About Fairness

Hello, My Name Is Scrambled Eggs by Jamie Gilson (New York: Lothrop, Lee & Shepard Books, 1985). Harvey tries to make his new Vietnamese friend into an American-style person. But Tuan has his own ideas. Ages 9–12.

Maniac Magee by Jerry Spinelli (New York: HarperCollins, 1992). A mysterious hero brings black and white citizens of the town together. Ages 7–12.

Stay Away from Simon! by Carol Carrick (Boston: Houghton Mifflin, 1991). After a mentally handicapped boy follows Lucy and her brother home one day, the children need to examine their fears and feelings. Ages 9–11.

The War With Grandpa by Robert Kimmel Smith (New York: Delacorte, 1984). Peter doesn't think it's fair that he has to give his bedroom to Grandpa, who comes to live with the family. Ages 9–11.

FORGIVENESS

Ché Butler-
Whitebear

Someone Who's Forgiving

Ché Butler-Whitebear Learns from His Ancestors
Otis, Oregon

"You look like a girl!" a tall boy said, pulling on Ché's long black hair. Eight-year-old Ché Butler-Whitebear knew he was a boy—a brave and strong one. He wanted to wear his hair long in the Native American way. Tempted to punch the tall boy's nose, Ché closed his fist. But he stopped himself. It wouldn't help.

A girl with a long red ponytail skipped up to Ché and said, "Indians were gone with the dinosaurs." She giggled.

Ché's cheeks felt hot as coals, but he thought of the peaceful teachings of his family and his grandfather, and didn't say anything. He just walked away.

Then his teacher said that the buffalo had died out because the Indians killed them all. When Ché heard this, he got mad. It wasn't true. He ran home and told his mother he didn't want to go back to the school.

Ché's mother understood. "Ché-Man," she said, "I will enroll you in a better school." Soon Ché was attending Neskowin Valley School. He loved this new school, where he studied and learned a great deal.

Ché loved his family even more than his new school—especially his younger brother, Budhah-Boy. Budhah-Boy was four and a half. Ché helped his brother dress and comb his hair, and wrestled playfully with him.

When Ché was nine years old, he and his brother and cousins were playing baseball under the tall pines by the Salmon River. Budhah accidentally got smacked in the head with the metal bat. His skin burst open above his eyebrow, and blood poured out. Ché walked his brother home to their white trailer house. There he put him in bed, stroked his long hair, and cared for him until the paramedic (health care worker) arrived to patch up Budhah's forehead.

Ché could forgive his cousin who had swung the metal bat. But he carried another sorrow in his heart. He missed his aunt and his brother Daniel, who had died when Ché was younger. He had called his aunt Auntie-Mom because she had been like a second mother to him. Ché didn't understand why the **Creator** had taken his loved ones to the spirit world when he needed them here on Earth.

Creator is a word some people use for God or a Higher Power.

Ché thought about the deaths of his loved ones. He remembered other hurts, too. He wanted to punch the kids at school who had made fun of him—and the teacher. Ché felt anger gnawing in his chest like a hungry bear. But the anger made his heart feel heavy.

He talked with his mother about it. "You believe in your **ancestors** and the Creator, don't you?" she asked.

Ancestors are people who came before and are now gone, such as great-grandparents and great-great-grandparents.

65

Ché nodded his head. He knew what he needed to do. He would fast—he wouldn't eat any food for a whole day. During this day of fasting, Ché danced and prayed to the Creator. The dust billowed around him like a cloud as his feet pounded the dirt. At the end of the day, he fell into bed. There, he had his answer. A voice as soft as feathers spoke to his heart. Ché should forgive everyone. He would let the Creator carry his burden. Suddenly, the drumbeats of his ancestors beat in Ché's chest, and his heart felt light and free.

Forgiveness—
What Does It Mean?

"It is by forgiving that one is forgiven."
—Mother Teresa

Eight-year-old Maria started school three weeks later than everyone else. This was because her parents were migrant farm workers, and they had to follow the crops. In August and September they picked tomatoes. And in the spring, Maria sometimes had to quit school early so her parents could go to California to pick grapes.

It seemed to Maria that all the kids at school already had friends. She felt like the last peach on the tree, when all the others had been picked. Worse, she saw kids looking at her hand-me-down (used) clothes. A girl named Crystal pointed at the large sneakers on Maria's feet and laughed. Two other girls poked fun at Maria's dress, which was faded and worn. All the rest of the girls wore new-looking jeans or pants.

One day Maria lost her temper when Crystal made fun of her. She got so mad that she shoved Crystal into a mud puddle on the playground. Crystal cried. Then all the girls and some boys smeared mud on Maria's dress.

That night Maria cried to her mom. But her mom only said, "Maria, remember that without the rocks, the stream would lose its song. Learn to **forgive,** Maria, and you will be forgiven."

Maria went back to school. She decided to stay calm. She ignored the teasing and quietly watched the kids around her. After awhile, she saw that Crystal didn't understand her math, so Maria helped her. She helped Everett, too. At lunch, Maria shared a ripe peach with Savannah. Then, at recess, Crystal asked Maria to hold one end of the jump rope. Soon Maria stopped feeling mad and lonely.

Someone has probably treated you unkindly. Maybe someone has told a lie about you, or cheated you, or taken your friends or homework, or told you that you were stupid. Or worse. It shouldn't ever happen, but it does.

What can you do when someone is mean or hurts you? Often, the best thing is to find a way to forgive the person. When you forgive someone, you give up your hurt or angry feelings. You stop blaming the person for being unkind. Part of **forgiveness** is saying "I forgive you." But forgiveness is more than that. When you truly forgive someone, you mean what you say. You let go of the hurt or angry thoughts you have about the person. You forgive the person not just with your words, but with your heart.

You might say, "But being mean is a bad thing to do. Why should I let someone get away with that?" Forgiveness doesn't have to mean that you do nothing when someone hurts you. You don't have to put up with it in silence, either. You can report what happened to a trusted adult, like a parent or teacher. But you can still forgive the person and leave your angry feelings behind.

When you forgive someone, you'll feel better inside. Think about it. When you're angry at someone, you might go around all day scowling, or feeling sad and grumpy. You might think about mean things to do back. What if you hurt someone back? Then you'll have something else to feel bad about. It doesn't feel very good to think mean or angry thoughts. All those bad feelings hurt you inside. They can even make you sick! Really letting go of the feelings can help you feel good inside.

"It's not that easy," you might say, and you'd be right. Becoming a forgiving person takes courage. But you'll be happier if you learn to forgive.

There are more reasons to show forgiveness to others. For one thing, people aren't as likely to pick on you anymore if they don't get a reaction. And when you forgive people, they see a new way to act. Maybe the next time they start to do something mean, they'll change their mind. Maybe they'll think about how good it felt to be forgiven.

How Can You Be Forgiving?

Sometimes before you can forgive someone you need to talk to an adult you trust. You might also need to let go of anger you're feeling. When you've done that, it's time to talk to the person who hurt you. By then, you may feel more ready to forgive the person. It's also important to forgive *yourself* when you've done something you're sorry about.

Talk to an Adult You Trust

Talk about what happened with an adult such as your mom, dad, or teacher. If someone has hurt you, don't ignore it or pretend it didn't happen. If the person broke a rule at school or at home, tell your teacher or parent. If the person hurt you *without* breaking a rule, you still may want to talk about it with a grown-up. Someone you trust can help you figure out what to do so you'll feel better.

Let Your Anger Go

Trying to get even is like throwing dry wood on a fire. The angry flames will leap higher and higher. The best way to stop a fight is to *stop fighting.* The best way to stop feeling mad is to drop your anger like a hot coal. Because if you don't, that anger will hurt you even more. Anger can make you sick. It can keep you from doing good things and cause you to lose friends.

You might be thinking, "How do I let my anger go?" There are lots of things you can do to let your anger out without hurting anyone or anything. Here are a few ideas:

- Write about how you feel, or draw an "angry picture."
- Role-play what happened and how angry you feel. Do this with a grown-up you feel safe and comfortable with.
- Get involved in a sport that lets you use all your energy, like soccer, basketball, tennis, or karate.
- Take a shower or bath to feel more relaxed.
- Rest, listen to quiet music, or take a nap.
- Do something you like to do. This can calm you and help you feel better.

- Exercise! Run, jump, skip, or hop as fast and as hard as you can.
- Punch your pillow. It won't get hurt, and it won't punch you back.

The "Cooperation" chapter has other suggestions for dealing with angry feelings on pages 46–48. If you need help, ask your dad, mom, teacher, or another adult.

Talk to the Person Who Hurt You

Learning to forgive doesn't mean you'll never stand up for yourself. It doesn't mean you let people keep hurting you. Tell the person how you feel. You don't need to use mean or angry words. For example, maybe your friend told something private about you to some kids at school. You could tell your friend, "I trusted you to keep that private. Now everyone's teasing me. I feel really hurt."

If you want, you can also say what you'd like the person to do to help make things right. Sometimes this is possible, and sometimes it isn't. You could say, "I'd like you to apologize." Or, "I need you to promise that you won't do this again."

Listen to what the person says. Sometimes people can be hurtful without meaning to. Give the person a chance to explain.

Forgive the Person

You might not feel ready to forgive the person right away. When you *are* ready, say, "I forgive you." If you mean it, you should feel at peace inside. Then try to do something nice for the person. This shows that you mean what you've said. You could say, "Would you like to share my snack?" Or, "Would you like me to save you a seat on the bus today?"

IMPORTANT!

It's important to be able to forgive. But sometimes there are bigger problems in a relationship. Maybe you have a friend who's mean all the time, or one who's leading you to do things you know you shouldn't do. Maybe someone else is hurting or scaring you. When that happens, to be safe, you may need to stop the relationship. You can ask your dad or mom or another grown-up you trust to help you figure out what to do.

Will your friend always be a good friend after that? Will she or he never hurt you again? You can't make that happen. But you can decide how *you* will act. You can decide to be forgiving.

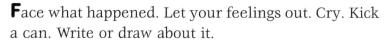

7 WAYS TO BE FORGIVING

Face what happened. Let your feelings out. Cry. Kick a can. Write or draw about it.

Open up your heart and give the person who has hurt you a chance to explain. It's possible she or he didn't mean to hurt you.

Report what happened. Tell the person who hurt you how you feel.

Get help from a trusted adult.

Imagine how the other person might feel.

Value the other person. Try to see what is good in the other person. Then do something nice for him or her, if you can. This is the hardest part, but it will make you stronger.

Erase what happened from your mind. Forget it. Only remember what you learned.

Forgive Yourself, Too

What if you're the one who has hurt someone else? You can't change what's happened, but you can learn from it. And you can decide to do the right thing now. Admit what you did. Don't lie to yourself or tell yourself it really wasn't important. Tell the person you're sorry. Ask what you can do to make it right. Think about how you want to act next time. If you need help because you feel bad or don't know what to do, talk to a grown-up you trust. Ask the person to help you find a way to forgive *yourself*.

WHEN YOU'RE SORRY— 5 WAYS TO FORGIVE YOURSELF

Say you're sorry.

Offer your friendship.

Repair what you did, if you can.

Resist doing it again. This can be hard, but keep trying.

Yank out your bad feelings like weeds, so there's room in your heart to forgive yourself.

What If?

Here are some situations for you to think about, write about, talk about, or act out.

1. Your friend tells a lie about you. How might you forgive your friend and stop the lie, too?

2. Your brother steals some money from your bedroom. You ask him to stop, but he keeps on stealing. What might you do to help him stop stealing? What can you do to help yourself forgive him?

3. One day, you get really angry at your best friend. Without thinking, you say something that hurts her feelings. You see the look on her face, and you wish you could take back every word. You do your best to apologize, and your friend says, "That's okay. No big deal." But you can't get that look out of your mind. And you can't believe you said

those awful words to someone you care about. Your friend has forgiven you. How can you forgive yourself?

FIND OUT MORE . . .

Here are two books to help you understand and deal with feelings that can hurt you inside and make it hard to forgive yourself and others:

Don't Rant and Rave on Wednesdays! The Children's Anger-Control Book by Adolph Moser, Ed.D. (Kansas City, MO: Landmark Editions, 1994). This book gives ideas on accepting and handling anger. Ages 6–9.

Don't Pop Your Cork on Mondays! The Children's Anti-Stress Book by Adolph Moser, Ed.D. (Kansas City, MO: Landmark Editions, 1988). **Stress** is worry that won't go away and that makes you feel bad. This is a fun book that looks at what causes stress and what stress does to you. Gives ideas on how you can keep stress from happening—and how to handle it when you can't. Ages 6–9.

"One of the secrets of a long and fruitful life is to forgive everybody everything every night before you go to bed."

—*Ann Landers*

More Ways to Learn to Be Forgiving

Here are some activities you can do to help you be able to forgive others—and yourself.

Unscramble an Important Idea

Solve this two-part puzzle and learn something important about forgiveness.

First, unscramble the letters to read a message. (The solution is at the bottom of the page.)

GOFIRNSEVES SI A EYK OT FENPSLUCESEA.

Next, think about what the message says. Do you think it's true? Why or why not? Explain your ideas to someone in your family or to a friend or classmate.

Start a "Here's What I Can Do" List

Here's what you'll need:

- Paper and pen or pencil

Do certain things push your "anger button"? At the top of a sheet of paper, write a few things that lead you to anger. You might use these starter ideas:

- I get mad when my friend . . .
- I get mad when my mom (or dad) . . .
- I get mad when my sister (or brother) . . .

Beneath your sentences, write, "Here's what I can do to control my anger." Write ideas for letting go of angry feelings. You'll find some ideas in this chapter and in the chapters on "Cooperation" and "Fairness." You can also talk to other adults and kids about ideas for getting rid of angry feelings.

FORGIVENESS IS A KEY TO PEACEFULNESS.

> I get mad when my stepmom makes me go to bed early.
>
> <u>Here's what I can do to control my anger:</u>
>
> Count to 10 and take deep breaths.
> Remember not to yell and cry.
> Talk to her and my dad together about it.

Find Words of Forgiveness

Think of words you can use to show forgiveness. Think of as many different things as you can. If you like, do this activity with a friend or with someone in your family. You might even want to role-play (act out) scenes where you could use the words. Here are some ideas to get you started:

Words for talking about what happened:
"You're nice to me when we're alone. I wish you'd act the same way when other people are around, too."

Words for forgiving someone else:
"I know you're sorry. I'm not mad anymore."

Words for forgiving yourself:
"I've learned from my mistake."

Draw What Happens

Here's what you'll need:
- Drawing paper
- Crayons, colored pencils, or markers

Draw pictures of good things that can happen when people show forgiveness. You might show two friends working on a project together instead of doing it alone. Or a family talking and laughing at supper instead of sitting silent and angry while they eat. You can think of other ideas. Hang your pictures someplace where they can remind you to be forgiving.

REMINDER:
Don't forget to keep track of your progress on the "Building My Character Muscles" chart (page 16).

Read Stories About Forgiving

Footprints Up My Back by Kristi Diane Hall (New York: Atheneum, 1984). A young girl who finds it impossible to say no is too quick to excuse the selfishness of others. She learns to be dependable without letting others use or hurt her. Ages 9–12.

Forgive the River, Forgive the Sky by Gloria Whelan (Grand Rapids, MI: William B. Eerdmans, 1999). A child cures her own hurt by helping an injured ex-pilot to break down his wall of anger. Ages 9–12.

I Did It, I'm Sorry by Caralyn Buehner (New York: Dial Books for Young Readers, 1998). A fun book of stories about animals who make mistakes and have to figure out what to do to fix things. Ages 4–8.

Lone Wolf by Kristine L. Franklin (Cambridge, MA: Candlewick Press, 1997). Perry's sister has died and his parents have divorced. Alone and unhappy, Perry lives with his dad. A new family moves in next door, reminding Perry of things he wants to forget. His friendship with the oldest girl helps him learn to accept and forgive his family. Ages 9–12.

Tough Loser by Barthe Declements (New York: Puffin, 1996). Nine-year-old Jenna cares for new puppies. She also tries to help her older brother overcome his temper, which threatens to ruin his chances of becoming a hockey star. Ages 9–12.

HONESTY

Claudia
Montes

Someone Who's Honest

Claudia Montes—Tortillas and Candy
Chiuhua, Mexico

When Claudia Montes was eight years old, her mother asked her to go to the store and buy some warm tortillas for the family's dinner. She gave Claudia **pesos** to buy them with. Claudia stuffed the pesos in her pocket and opened the door of her two-room **adobe** house. Behind the house, beautiful mesquite trees grew across the lavender hills. She skipped along the dirt road, while the sun shone down on her black hair.

The store was a small house with one room for selling tortillas and candy. The woman told Claudia she'd have to wait a few minutes for warm tortillas. Claudia eyed the candy. It looked so tasty! She wrapped her fist around the pesos in her pocket. Why not buy the candy instead and make up a story to tell her mother?

Pesos are a type of money used in Mexico and other Spanish-speaking countries.

An **adobe** house is made of clay or sun-dried earth.

77

Claudia's mouth watered as she pointed at some sugary suckers and red-hot candies. She spent all of the money on candy. It tasted yummy, but on the way home, she didn't feel happy inside.

When Claudia opened the door to her adobe house, her mother asked her, "Where are the tortillas?"

Claudia hid the candies behind her back, but she couldn't lie. Instead, she told the truth. Her mother told Claudia to stand beside the house to think about it. Claudia didn't mind standing beside the house, because she was glad she had told the truth. She felt much better.

A year later, when Claudia was at her school, San Francisco Y Madero, her honesty was tested again. While the teacher was out of the room, a boy placed a sack of apricots on the teacher's desk as a gift. One of the boys near the front grabbed the sack and broke an apricot in half. He laughed and stuffed the fruit in his mouth. Then he passed the plastic sack around, and other kids grabbed apricots, broke them in half, and shared them. The boy who brought the apricots said nothing, probably because he didn't want the kids to make fun of him.

Claudia watched, but she didn't take any apricots. "This isn't honest," she thought.

When the teacher came in, he didn't know what had happened, because he never saw the bag.

But Claudia spoke up. "They ate your apricots," she told the teacher. She told the whole story in front of the class.

Claudia's classmates lied and told the teacher they hadn't eaten any. They said that Claudia had eaten some apricots. Claudia's cheeks burned. She knew it was right to tell the truth, but she felt terrible.

The teacher punished the whole class. For the next few days afterward, some of Claudia's friends ignored her. Others asked her why she told on them. Some kids refused to play with her. But Claudia didn't worry. She still had friends who respected her. Claudia understood something important: Even though telling the truth can sometimes lead to trouble, inside it hurts less than telling a lie.

Honesty—What Does It Mean?

"Honesty's the best policy."

—Cervantes

When my sister Pat turned twelve, she was supposed to start paying a dime for a bus ride. The next time she road the bus, the bus driver gave her a nickel back for her dime. Pat was shy and afraid to say anything. She thought to herself, "I'm twelve now, and I should pay a dime." But she *didn't* tell the driver.

Instead she went home and asked our father what he would do. Dad answered, "I'm not going to do anything. It's up to you. You could probably keep paying a nickel for a long time without anyone knowing it." Dad patted her shoulder and said, "The bus company won't go broke from losing your nickels. But the way I look at it, I'm not sure it's worth it to sell your **honesty** for a nickel."

The next time my sister boarded the bus, she handed the bus driver fifteen cents—a dime for that day and a nickel for the other time.

That was many years ago, and my father has long since died. Recently I went to a bank drive-up window and gave the bank teller a check for $1,500 to put in my savings account. The busy woman made a mistake and gave me two things: a receipt for $1,500 *and* $1,500 in cash. Now my account had $1,500, and I had another $1,500 in my hand. By accident, the clerk had doubled my money! But in the back of my mind, I remembered my father's words. And I said to myself, "No, Dad. I wouldn't sell my honesty either— not for a nickel, and not for $1,500." I gave the money back to the teller.

These stories tell you something about what it means to be **honest.** When you're honest, you don't steal. You don't cheat other people, even if *they* make a mistake, not you. Being honest also means that you don't lie—you're always truthful.

Is it always easy to be honest? No. In the end, though, being honest is the right thing to do for yourself and for the people around you.

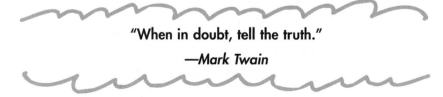

"When in doubt, tell the truth."

—*Mark Twain*

6 GOOD REASONS TO TELL THE TRUTH

1. Telling the truth lets everyone know what really happened.

2. Telling the truth keeps people from being blamed for something they didn't do.

3. You usually get into less trouble when you tell the truth than when you get caught lying.

4. Your friends, family, and teachers will trust and respect you more if you tell the truth.

5. It's easier to tell the truth. You don't have to remember a bunch of lies to keep your story straight.

6. Telling the truth helps you to feel calm and peaceful inside.

How Can You Be Honest?

There are three important things to think about when it comes to being honest: being truthful, being the real you, and being **trustworthy.**

Be Truthful

You probably know what it means to lie outright. If you cut your sister's bangs and then tell your dad, "I didn't do it," that's a lie. If you steal candy from the store and tell your friend you paid for it, that's a lie. If you didn't do your homework but tell the teacher you accidentally lined the birdcage with it, that's a lie. You know it's wrong to tell lies—even if the truth will get you in trouble.

But sometimes people tell "little white lies." Even though it's small, a teeny-tiny lie is still a lie, just like a lie that's a big whopper.

Suppose your teacher tells you that if you read each night for fifteen minutes, you'll get a star on your chart at school. What if you forget to read your book one night? Is it okay to tell the teacher that you read it anyway? "After all," you might think, "it's only a little lie. I can probably read fifteen minutes extra some other night to make up for it. No one will know the difference, will they?" The truth is, your teacher may not know, but *you'll* know.

There's always one person who's hurt by a "little white lie." That person is you. Each time you lie, it gets easier to lie the next time. Each time you tell the truth—even when it's really hard to do—your truth muscles get stronger. That makes it easier to tell the truth the next time.

**"That's one of the troubles with a lie.
You've got to keep adding to it to make it believable to people."**
—Bertrand R. Brinley

You might be thinking, "Does that mean I should tell my grandma I don't like the jacket she gave me for my birthday?" That's a good question. There are times when the most important thing is to be kind. Even then, you don't have to lie. For example, maybe you don't like the jacket even though it's your favorite color, green. You could say, "Thanks, Grandma. Green's my favorite color."

Be Genuine

Being **genuine** means being the real you. When you're genuine, you *are* what you *say* you are. You don't take your brother's trophy he won at the town bike race and tell everyone he's the world biking champion. You don't tell your teacher that you wrote a poem yourself when really your sister is the one who wrote it. You don't tell your new friend that your dad died when the truth is that he and your mom are divorced and he lives in another city.

Being genuine means that you don't live a lie. The *real* you is the one people see and hear. Sometimes people have a hard time being themselves. They're afraid other people won't like them. But people who care about you want to know the real you. They want to know they can trust you to be what you say you are. This lets them act like themselves around you. It lets *them* be real, too.

Be Trustworthy

If you tell your mom you'll make your bed before you go to school, and you do it, she'll know she can trust you. If you tell your teacher you'll bring a pencil to school each day, and you do it, he'll know he can trust you. By doing what you say you'll do, you earn your mom's and teacher's trust. "But wait," you might say. "What's that got to do with honesty?" Everything. Because being trustworthy means keeping your word. It means you do the best you can to do the things you promise to do.

Being trustworthy means that people can count on you to do the things you say you'll do. When you're trustworthy, your parents, teachers, and youth leaders will respect you. As their respect grows, they'll probably give you more privileges. Your friends will respect you more, too, because they'll know they can count on you.

**"Friends gotta trust each other . . .
cause ain't nothin' like a true friend."**

—Mildred D. Taylor

Before you make up a story or answer a question with a lie, play "Stop! Think! Go!"

→ Don't say anything for a moment or two.

→ What really happened? What might happen if you don't tell the truth?

→ Go ahead and speak the truth.

6 WAYS TO BE AN HONEST PERSON

Hold on to the real you. Make sure your family, teachers, and friends know that you're genuine—always truthful about who you are.

Own up to mistakes that you make, even if you're afraid you'll get in trouble. Remember that lying leads to even more trouble.

Never keep silent when it's important to tell the truth. When you know about a lie and don't say anything, you're letting the lie live on. Turn a silent lie into a loud truth by speaking up.

Earn people's trust by keeping your promises to them and by never cheating or stealing. Take back anything you borrow, and never take anything without asking.

Stop and think about what really happened so you can tell it truthfully. Also think about what might happen if you *don't* tell the truth.

Tell your dad or mom, your teacher, or another adult you trust that you've made a promise to always tell the truth.

What If?

Here are some situations for you to think about, write about, talk about, or act out.

1. At a grocery store, you pay the cashier for some ice cream, and he gives you back too much change. There's a long line of people waiting, and you can tell the cashier wants you to hurry. Should you tell him and return the extra change? Would it depend on how much money you got back? Would you tell him if he gave you a nickel too much? A dollar? Ten dollars? How would you decide?

2. Your mom and stepdad don't like you or your brother to eat candy without permission. You know that your brother has a sack of candy hidden in the corner of his closet. He tells you that if you'll keep his secret, he'll share the candy with you. Should you go along and enjoy the candy? Not take any candy and say nothing? Speak up to your mom and stepdad? Since you're not the one hiding the candy, does it matter if you say nothing? Why or why not?

3. Your older sister has a fancy, expensive watch she bought with money she earned from her part-time job. She lets you wear the watch to school for a party. Your friends think it's your watch, and they're impressed. They gather around you and look at you with wide eyes. Someone says, "You must be rich to have a watch like that." You know you're not rich, but it feels good to have everyone think so. What will happen if you tell the truth? If you don't? Does it matter in a case like this? Why or why not?

> "Anastasia wasn't crazy about telling lies, even to herself; she did it, sometimes, but it always gave her a stomachache."
>
> **—Lois Lowry**

More Ways to Be Honest

Here are some activities you can do to find more ways to be honest.

Talk About "Living a Lie"

Have you ever heard the phrase "to live a lie"? Talk with your family about what it might mean. Start by thinking of examples of *how* people might live a lie. (For instance, someone who's not a fast runner might claim to be one. Someone might say he or she has been to Africa when this isn't true.) Then talk about all the reasons *why* someone might make up a story like this. What could happen when other people start to ask questions about the story? What can happen to your body and your mind if you try to live a lie?

Ask your parents if they ever lived a lie when they were younger. What happened? How did they feel? How far did it go? How could they have been honest instead?

(This is a good activity for a family meeting. To learn about starting family meetings, see "Have Family Meetings," pages 37–38.)

Watch TV Commercials

 Can you trust everything you see and hear on television? With a parent or another adult, spend an hour watching TV. Focus on the commercials. Are they honest? Use questions like these to judge how honest each commercial is:

- What extreme words does the ad use? (Listen for words like *perfect, never, only, always,* and *the best.* There's usually not just one product that's best, even if a company claims that its is.)
- Does the ad offer proof about how great the product is? Does it say what expert (such as a doctor or an athlete) tested the product? Is it an expert you can trust?

- Does the ad give any warnings about the product? (For example, "This toy has tiny parts that small children can choke on.") Should it?
- What else do you notice about the ad's honesty?

Read Fables About Honesty

Fables are stories that have been told to children for a very long time. A fable usually teaches a lesson. "The Honest Woodman," "The Indian Cinderella," and "The Boy Who Cried 'Wolf'" are three fables that teach about honesty. You'll find others, too, depending on what book of fables you read. As you read, think about questions like these:

- How was the story important to people in the past?
- Why is the story important to you now?
- What other character traits does the story teach about?
- Does the story lead you to want to work on being more honest? In what ways?

FIND OUT MORE . . .
The Children's Book of Virtues by William J. Bennett (New York: Simon & Schuster, 1995). This is a recent version of some fables and tales, including "The Honest Woodman," "The Indian Cinderella," and "The Boy Who Cried 'Wolf.'"

Read About Honest People in Real Life

Read about real people who were (or are) known for being honest. Ask your parents or grandparents, your teacher, a leader or teacher at your place of worship, or a librarian or media specialist for ideas.

FIND OUT MORE . . .

Two famous Americans who were known for their honesty were Abraham Lincoln (known as "Honest Abe") and George Washington. Check out these books about Lincoln and Washington:

Abe Lincoln Goes to Washington, 1837–1865 by Cheryl Harness (Washington, DC: National Geographic Society, 1997). Tells of Lincoln's life in Congress and as president during the Civil War. Includes maps and illustrations. There's also an earlier book about Lincoln by the same author: *Young Abe Lincoln: The Frontier Days, 1809–1837* (Washington, DC: National Geographic Society, 1996). Ages 6–12.

Honest Abe by Edith Kunhardt (New York: Mulberry Paperback Books, 1998). Tells the story of Abraham Lincoln's life from when he lived in a log cabin to when he went to the White House. Ages 4–8.

Crossing the Delaware: A History in Many Voices by Louise Peacock (New York: Atheneum, 1998). Read about Washington's role in the Revolutionary War through the stories of a soldier and writings of the time. Though the reading level is for ages 9–12, all ages will enjoy this book.

From Colonies to Country with George Washington by Deborah Hedstrom (Sisters, OR: Multanomah, 1997). Booming cannons, whispered death plots, and a submarine make the Revolutionary War a reality. This book is part of the "My American Journey" series. Includes collector cards, a character-development booklet on leadership, and copies of 1776 documents. Ages 10 and up.

REMINDER:
Don't forget to keep track of your progress on the "Building My Character Muscles" chart (page 16).

Write Your Own Fable

Make up your own fable about honesty. You could make something up right from the start, or you could rewrite a fable you know. For example, a fable called "The Girl Who Cried 'Fire!'" could be based on "The Boy Who Cried 'Wolf.'" Can you think of others? You can write the fable on your own, with a friend or classmate, or with someone in your family.

"A lie comes back sooner or later."

—African proverb

Read Stories About Honesty

Angel in Charge by Judy Dalton (New York: Houghton Mifflin, 1985). When Angel's mom goes on vacation, everything falls apart. Angel lies about things to her mother and her teacher, fearing she and her brother might be put in a foster home. Ages 8–10.

A Day's Work by Eve Bunting (New York: Clarion Books, 1997). Francisco helps his grandfather find work as a gardener by lying about his grandfather's skills. Grandfather's strong sense of honesty sets things straight. Ages 5–8.

Sam, Bangs, and Moonshine by Evaline Ness (New York: Henry Holt & Company, 1987). Sam keeps telling wild stories ("moonshine") until they get her friend and her cat into trouble. Ages 4–8.

213 Valentines by Barbara Cohen (New York: Henry Holt & Company, 1991). When Wade is put in a fourth-grade class for gifted and talented kids, he doesn't adjust very well. He decides to send himself 213 valentines signed with the names of famous people. Ages 7–10.

Your Move, J.P. by Lois Lowry (New York: Dell, 1991). J.P. goes out of his way to impress his new "crush." Things get complicated after a simple lie gets out of control. Ages 9–13.

Zach Zirkle (left) and his brother Isaiah

Someone Who Cares About His Brother and Friend

Zach Zirkle Protects His Brother
Spokane, Washington

Eight-year-old Zach Zirkle wound up his arm and shot a snowball straight into the middle of a group of neighbor kids. They all had joined together for a snowball fight in the deep snow in front of Zach's house. Zach's older sister and his seven-year-old brother Isaiah joined in the fun. Isaiah and Zach shared a bedroom and were best friends. Although Zach and his brother were the youngest kids throwing snowballs, they aimed straight and hit their targets.

But the fun soon turned mean. Isaiah teased the older kids, claiming they couldn't throw as straight as he could. The two oldest, biggest kids got mad. They charged at Isaiah, knocked him into the snowbank, and began kicking him in the back and ribs.

Zach's older sister screamed at them to stop. The other kids watched in shock, but the two bullies kept on with their cruel kicking and beating. Zach's sister ran into the house to find her mother.

Zach jumped at the bullies and tried to knock them off his little brother. He grabbed their arms and waists and yanked. Since the bullies were big fifth and sixth graders, they only laughed and shoved Zach to the ground.

Zach heard Isaiah gasp and cry out with choking sobs. The small boy couldn't get away from the repeated kicks of the bullies' heavy boots.

Zach paused just a second. Then he pulled himself to his hands and knees, crawled over to Isaiah, and threw his body over his little brother. He cradled his arms and legs around Isaiah to shield him from the terrible beating. The heavy kicks landed on Zach's sides and back instead. He closed his eyes and gritted his teeth against the painful blows.

Then something strange happened. After a few more heavy kicks, the two bullies backed off. Surprised at what Zach had done, they turned and ran away.

Zach tried to lift his little brother, but Isaiah could hardly move. Since Zach was ten pounds heavier than Isaiah, he was able to pull his brother up. Isaiah whimpered. Zach put his little brother's arm around his own neck and half carried, half dragged Isaiah to the house, where their mom and sister hurried out to meet them.

Isaiah had many bad bruises on his back and ribs from the attack but, because of Zach, he didn't have more serious injuries. Zach's great love for Isaiah gave him the courage to take the blows for his little brother and best friend.

Vicious means dangerously cruel and hurtful. When someone does something vicious, he or she wants to hurt someone very badly.

IMPORTANT!

What the older kids did to Isaiah was **vicious.** It was against the law. When people hurt others like this, they need help. Maybe you or someone you know is being hurt in this way. Or maybe you've hurt someone or are afraid you might. It's important to talk to an adult you trust. Tell the person what's happening or what you're worried about. This is an important thing you can do to keep yourself and others from being hurt.

Relationship— What Does It Mean?

"Never again fail to come to the aid of someone we love."

—*Robert Joseph Burch*

In 1996, a three-year-old boy fell into a gorilla cage at the Brookfield Zoo. He didn't mean to. He climbed an 18-foot railing and toppled into the cage. When he landed, he was knocked out. A mother gorilla named Binti Jua was carrying her baby on her back. She hurried over to the boy, picked him up, and cradled him in her arms. Then she carried him over to the cage door and gently placed him on the floor. She stood there and protected him from the other gorillas until a zoo worker came and took the boy out.

It's natural for mothers to love and protect their own babies. But zoo visitors were surprised at what the mother gorilla had done for a human child. No one could find out why she did that, because it's hard to talk to a gorilla.

You probably first learned about love from your mother or another person who cared for you when you were very young. The closeness between you and this loving person was your first **relationship.** As you grew, you formed ties with other people in your **family,** with people who cared for you, and with people in your neighborhood, school, community, and place of worship.

Today, you have relationships with many people. Two of the most important kinds of relationships you have are with your family and your **friends.** In this chapter, you'll learn ideas for starting and building strong relationships with family and friends. You'll also look at a third relationship—the one you have with yourself.

IMPORTANT!

What if you don't feel loved and cared for? If you don't feel that you have a safe and loving relationship with at least one adult, seek help from another adult you trust. This might be a relative, neighbor, teacher, school counselor, or youth leader. Keep looking until you find someone to help.

How Can You Build Strong Relationships?

Forming good relationships with family and friends will help you be a more happy, peaceful person. Relationships work two ways, so your friends and family will probably feel happier and more peaceful, too.

One of the best ways to build relationships is by spending time together. The next few pages are full of ideas for ways you can spend time with family and friends. As you try the ideas, keep in mind what you're learning about building your character muscles. All of the character traits in *Being Your Best* can help you have fun and get along with your parents, brothers and sisters, and friends. Traits like honesty, caring, cooperation, and respect help you be a better friend and family member.

If there are problems in one of your relationships, take time to talk them over. Remember to listen, share your feelings, and work to find a way to fix what's wrong. (To learn more about solving problems, see "Use TALKS to Solve a Problem" on pages 45–46.)

Have Fun with Your Family

"It isn't walls and furniture that make a home. It's the family."
—*Natalie Savage Carlson*

What makes a family? A family is the person or people you live with. People in a family love and take care of each other. You might live in one family, or you might live in two. Your family might have lots of people, or just a few. Moms, dads, stepparents, guardians, foster parents, uncles, aunts, grandparents, sisters, brothers, cousins, special friends—any of these might be part of your family. Some families include people of different races and colors. Family members don't always live together. But even if you're away from people in your family, you can still have a relationship.

Whether your family is big or small, you can help build a strong relationship if you take time to have some fun together. Here are some ideas:

- Play games together. Some families like board games, card games, charades, or Twenty Questions. It can be fun to learn new games together, too.
- Make yourselves into a human sculpture by wrapping your arms and legs together.
- Make trails for miniature cars all through your home or around the yard. Play with the cars together.
- Play ball, tag, or hide-and-seek.
- Tell stories. Ask your grandparents, parents, aunts, and uncles to tell you what it was like when they were young.

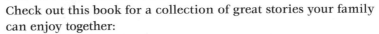

FIND OUT MORE . . .

Check out this book for a collection of great stories your family can enjoy together:

Hey! Listen to This: Stories to Read Aloud edited by Jim Trelease (New York: Penguin USA, 1992). This book has fifty read-aloud chapters from books like *Charlotte's Web, Ozma of Oz, Ramona the Pest, James and the Giant Peach*, and *Gentle Ben*. Stories to share in families with kids ages 5 and up.

- Plan a once-a-week family fun time. Watch a video together. Tell a story. Have a picnic on the patio or porch. One way to have weekly family time is with a family meeting. You can learn more by reading "Have Family Meetings" on pages 37–38.
- Bake a cake together and take it to a neighbor or a grandparent.
- Go biking, in-line skating, skiing, or swimming together.
- Hike or walk together.
- Sing or dance. Ask family adults to show you how to do "old days" dances.
- Have a pillow fight or a water fight. (The water fight is *outdoor* fun.)

- Make family rules. Believe it or not, it can be fun to do this together. You might make rule setting part of a family meeting.
- Make a family job chart. Choose the jobs each person will do. (See "Make a Cooperative Chores Chart," page 51, and "Make Family Chores Fair," pages 61–62.)
- Write a family motto. A motto is something your family stands for, such as "We're a together family," "We're a jogging family," or "We're a sing-along family."
- Plant flowers or a garden. Enjoy weeding, watering, and watching your garden grow.
- Start a family journal or photo album.

FIND OUT MORE . . .

Here are a few books that talk about different kinds of families and how the people in them can get along together:

Free to Be You and Me: And Free to Be . . . a Family (25th Anniversary Edition) by Marlo Thomas (Philadelphia, PA: Running Press, 1998). Stories, songs, poems, and pictures in a fun-filled book for kids and their families. Ages 7–12.

Dr. Ruth Talks About Grandparents: Advice for Kids on Making the Most of a Special Relationship by Ruth K. Westheimer (New York: Farrar, Straus & Giroux, 1997). Dr. Ruth, who lost both her parents and grandparents when she was ten, shares many ways grandparents and kids can enjoy and learn from each other. Ages 9–12.

Families: Poems Celebrating the African American Experience by Dorothy S. Strickland (Honesdale, PA: Boyds Mills Press, 1996). Illustrated poems for all children about family life by many different black writers. Ages 5–8.

In My Family/En Mi Familia by Carmen Lomas Garza (San Francisco, CA: Children's Book Press, 1996). A book of paintings with family stories about Mexican-American family life. Written in both English and Spanish. Ages 6–10.

This Is Me and My Two Families: An Awareness Scrapbook/ Journal for Children Living in Stepfamilies by Marla D. Evans and Rick Schuster (Washington, DC: American Psychological Association, 1991). A book to use with a parent or stepparent. Ages 9–12.

7 WAYS FAMILIES CAN BUILD A STRONGER HOME

Find ways to have fun. Forgive each other when you need to, and face your problems together.

Accept each other the way you are.

Make rules together. Plan jobs and work together, too.

Include each other in the things you do.

Listen and talk together.

Improve together and grow.

Explore and play together.

Serve and support each other. Do kind things for each other.

Have Fun with Your Friends

"And in the sweetness of friendship let there be laughter, and sharing of pleasures."

—*Kahlil Gibran*

A friend is someone you care about and like to do things with. There are many different kinds of friends. You might have some friends you've known and played with since you were little and others you met at school. Maybe you have friends you see only at your place of worship or at a club meeting. You might have friends of different ages in your apartment or neighborhood. Maybe you have a brother or sister who's also a friend.

Some people have lots of friends. Others have a few close ones. Think about you. Did you take the "What's My Personal Style?" quiz on page 9? That quiz probably told you something about whether you like to be with lots of friends or just a few.

How can you be a good friend? Many of the character traits you're learning will help you do this. When you're a good friend, you care about your friend. You treat him or her kindly, and with respect. You're fair and honest with your friend. You don't say mean things behind your friend's back. You do your best to get along, and when you disagree, you try to solve your problem together. If your friend does something that hurts you, you talk about it together. Remember that the best way to make and keep friends is by being a good friend yourself.

6 TIPS FOR MAKING AND KEEPING FRIENDS

1. Be accepting. Enjoy your friends for who they are.

2. Be a good listener.

3. Develop interest in others instead of talking only about yourself.

4. Be honest.

5. When there's work to be done, do your share.

6. Reach out to get to know new people. Don't always wait for someone else to take this first step.

You have a chance to make new friends every day. And you have a chance to build your relationships with the friends you already have. One of the best ways to build friendships is by having fun together. Here are some things you and your friends might enjoy:

- Fill up an old sock with sand, tie a knot in the opening, and play catch. The more socks, the merrier—it's fun to twirl the sock and see how high it goes when you throw it. (This is *outdoor* fun, of course!)
- Chase butterflies or grasshoppers.
- Make friends with a neighbor who enjoys birdwatching. Feed the birds together. Learn their names and how to identify them.
- Make crowns out of flowers or leaves.
- Hold an arm-wrestling contest.
- Roll down hills.
- Hold a laughing contest.

"It's so much more friendly with two."

—A.A. Milne

- Make rock "buddies." Decorate rocks with stick-on eyes and paper feet, then paint them.
- Bake cookies and take them to your school or club to share. Or take them to someone who just moved into your apartment or neighborhood.
- Have a party where you share your favorite books or perform or listen to music together.
- With a friend, read aloud to little kids. Take turns reading, or share the reading by taking different parts or characters in the story.

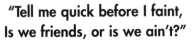

**"Tell me quick before I faint,
Is we friends, or is we ain't?"**

—Anonymous folk poem

- Read with an older person. She or he might read to you, or you might do the reading. Ask your senior friend to tell you stories, too.
- Save seeds from fruits and vegetables. Plant them.
- Build castles of sand or snow.
- With the help of an adult, find a tree that's safe to climb. Sit in the branches and view the world together from your perch high in the sky.
- Hold a bike-riding contest where you race and do stunts. (Wear helmets, and ask a grown-up to supervise.)
- Ask an adult to take you and a friend shopping. Together, find and buy a holiday or birthday gift for a friend. Another fun idea is to window-shop (to look but not buy). Compare what things cost, choose a "fantasy" outfit, or check out the latest styles so you can make them at home.
- Learn to juggle together. Then juggle water balloons (another game for outside).
- Take baby photos to class and try to guess who's who.

- Make paper chains and hang them around your rooms.
- Rake leaves into a pile, then jump in.
- Make a scrapbook or diary of all the things you've done together.

7 BUILDING BLOCKS FOR STRONG FRIENDSHIPS

Find out all you can about each other. Be friendly, fair, and forgiving.

Respect each other and act responsibly. Remember birthdays. Read together.

Include others. Share your interests. Imagine together.

Explore and enjoy things together.

Need each other. Be nice. Never lie or be unkind.

Depend on each other. Dare to dream and develop your interests together.

Share yourself, your family, and your friends with other people. Sing together. Smile.

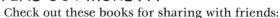

FIND OUT MORE . . .

Check out these books for sharing with friends:

The Absolutely True, Positively Awesome Book About . . . Me!!! by Me!!! (with Help from Jessica Wilber) (Minneapolis: Free Spirit Publishing, 1999). You and your friend might enjoy a friendship journal—a book where you write back and forth to each other. Learn more about this kind of journaling in a book written by school-age author Jessica Wilber. Though Jessica wrote the book with girls in mind, many of the ideas are great for girls *and* boys. Ages 6–10.

That's What a Friend Is by P.K. Hallinan (Nashville, TN: Ideals Childrens Books, 1981). A short and lighthearted book about the meaning of friendship. All ages.

Have Fun by Yourself

*"When you feel good about yourself,
others will feel good about you, too."*

—Jake Steinfeld

Did you know that your very best friend is *you*? Take some time to get to know yourself a little better. The better you can "get along" with yourself, the better your relationships with others will be. Here are some ways to enjoy time spent alone:

- Find a quiet, secret place in your home where you can just think. Your thinking place might be up in the attic, down in the basement, outside in a tree, on the porch or patio, under your bed, or in your closet.
- Start or write in a journal. Your journal might be a book where you write your dreams and feelings. It might be a log where you keep track of baseball scores and plays. It might be a notebook where you write letters to yourself, sketch pictures, or keep lists of things to do.
- Dress up in your parents' or grandparents' old clothes.
- Practice something you want to learn, like doing magic tricks, playing the trumpet, shooting baskets, or dancing.
- Make a dough creature. You can make your own dough: Mix 2 cups of flour, 1 cup of salt, 1 table-spoon of oil, a few drops of food coloring, and just enough water to keep the dough moist. Store unused dough in a tightly sealed plastic bag. After your creature sets (hardens), paint it with tempera paint.

- Draw or paint. Come up with your own pictures or copy something from a comic book, newspaper, or magazine. If you like, get a book from the library that shows you how to draw people, nature scenes, or building designs.
- Read. What do you like to read? Adventure series? Science fiction? Magazines on collecting things? Stories about real people (biographies)? Stories that are made up (fiction)? Comic books? Nature stories? Puzzle books? Try different things till you find something that's right for you.

"A book is a friend."
—American proverb

- Lie on your bed and listen to music. Or lie in the grass and watch clouds. Let yourself dream.
- Try a recipe from a cookbook, or make up a new recipe. How about pickles in potato pancakes? (Be sure to get permission first, and clean up the mess.)
- Make a playhouse out of boxes, sheets, and towels. Ask if you can eat your lunch in your playhouse.
- Make a basketball hoop out of an old tire or coat hanger. Have an adult or older friend help you hang it from a tree or post.
- Look under your bed. What's hiding there? It might be old socks, last week's sandwich, or a game you thought you'd lost. Clean up what you find. Then do the rest of your room.
- Start a collection of bottle caps, buttons, flowers, dolls, toy cars, or whatever interests you.
- Find out where you can take old newspapers, cans, plastic bottles, glass jars, and cardboard. Set up a recycling center for your household with boxes or sacks to save things in.

What If?

Here are some situations for you to think about, write about, talk about, or act out.

1. You want to be a better friend to your sister. But she says you're a pest, and she doesn't seem to want to be friends. How might you help your sister enjoy your company?

2. You have two friends who fight over you. They each want you to be their friend alone. You want to be friends with both. Is it possible to do that? What can you do or say to your friends?

3. There's someone in your class no one wants to be around. You feel sorry for the person, but you want to be with your own friends. Is it possible for you to become friends with the person and still keep your other friends? What can you do?

4. Your mom sends you to your room all the time. You don't like being sent to your room. What might you do to work things out better with your mom?

More Ways to Build Relationships

Here are some more activities you can do to help build strong relationships with friends and family.

Plan a "Special Guest" Dinner

Here's what you'll need:

- Paper and pens, colored pencils, or markers for making invitations and place cards
- *If you wish:* Tape recorder and cassette tape

Ask your mom or dad to help you plan a special dinner for a favorite relative or family friend. This is a nice event to plan for a grandparent. Set the date and time and send an invitation. Decide on the food and help with the shopping and cooking. Make place cards to put by each person's plate. At the dinner, ask your guest to tell stories from his or her life. If your guest doesn't mind, tape-record the stories. After dinner, share more stories or play a game together. Later, you might even want to write down one of the stories and present it to the guest.

Surprise Someone

Plan a surprise for a friend or family member. Make a bed. Wash dishes. Fold laundry. Give a small treat. Leave a note with your surprise.

Thanks for all the things you do.
Here is something nice for you.
It's now your turn to help another:
Father, mother, sister, brother.
Pass this note with your surprise
To help our family build strong ties.

From Kate

Go on a "Penny Ride"

Here's a fun activity to do with your family (you might invite a friend to come, too). Ask your dad or mom to take your family on a ride in the car. Bring along a penny. After you get on the street, take turns flipping the penny. If the penny comes up "heads," turn right at the end of the next street. If the penny turns up "tails," turn left at the next street. You can decide how many blocks to go before you flip the coin. A penny ride will take you surprising places. You can even try to get the penny to take you somewhere fun—like to the ice-cream store! (Flip the penny to decide who gets to choose where you'll go.) If your family doesn't have a car, you can take a "penny walk" together.

REMINDER: Don't forget to keep track of your progress on the "Building My Character Muscles" chart (page 16).

Start a "What Makes a Good Friend?" List

Here's what you'll need:
- Paper and pen or pencil

What goes into being a good friend? Write down words that tell the traits of a good friend (*for example:* friendly, not jealous, honest, likes to laugh). Think of as many qualities as you can. Then go back over your list and circle the qualities *you* have. Put a check mark next to traits you need to work on. How will you practice being a better friend? Keep your list close by (maybe inside your desk, journal, or closet door) where it can remind you of what it takes to be a good friend.

Read Stories About Relationships

Out of the Dust by Karen Hesse (New York: Scholastic, 1997). Fourteen-year-old Billie Jo survives her hard life in the Oklahoma dust bowl (when there were years with no rain) in the 1930s. Her mother dies, and the community turns against Billie Jo. Through her loss and sadness, Billie Jo learns an important truth about herself. Ages 9–12.

The View from Saturday by E.L. Konigsburg (New York: Atheneum, 1996). Four smart, shy twelve-year-olds are chosen to be on the Academic Bowl team. The book is filled with surprises as they learn about themselves and each other in this story of friendship. Ages 9–12.

Youn Hee & Me by C.S. Adler (Orlando, FL: Harcourt Brace, 1995). Caitlin loves her adopted Korean brother Simon. When the family learns that Simon has a sister in a Korean orphanage, they decide to adopt her, too. But Caitlin's disappointed in her new sister Youn Hee. And Youn Hee has trouble getting used to the United States. Slowly, they all come together as a family. Ages 8–12.

You're Not My Best Friend Anymore by Charlotte Pomerantz (New York: Dial Books for Young Readers, 1998). Two best friends live in a two-family house. When a big disagreement splits them apart, they find a way to work things out. Ages 8–10.

RESPECT

Sowon Bahk

Someone Who Respects Herself and Others

Sowon Bahk Shows Respect to Her Elders
Chinju, Korea

Sowon Bahk was seven years old when she and six friends decided to cook rice in her apartment. The idea sounded like so much fun that Sowon forgot she wasn't supposed to cook without an adult. In the process of cooking, the kids spilled rice and water all over the counter and onto the wooden floor. Before they could clean it up, Sowon's mother came home.

Her mother was very angry. "You must all go home," she said to Sowon's friends. She sent Sowon to her room.

Later, Sowon had to go back into the kitchen to clean up the mess. She felt bad, but she didn't talk back to her mom because Sowon had learned to respect her parents.

Sowon's father taught at the university. Often, the family entertained other teachers from the United States. The visitors admired Sowon's apartment. The red brick building was surrounded by beautiful flowers—red, yellow, purple, and pink—and stood next to a gently flowing stream.

"When these people come," her father told Sowon and her brother Yongsoo, "you must shake their hands like this. And you must smile and look into their eyes. This is polite, and it shows respect."

At school, Sowon learned to respect teachers. One day, as she and her thirty-five classmates cleaned the room after school, a boy began banging a broom up and down on the floor, mashing the straw bristles. The teacher returned and punished the boy.

Sowon knew that the boy who had been disrespectful would have to work hard to earn back the teacher's trust. That would take a long time. Sowon vowed she would never show disrespect to her teachers. Instead, she would respect them and speak to them in the formal way she had been taught. Because of this, Sowon's teachers respected her, too. They allowed her to take part in many activities.

Elders are people who are older than you, like your teachers or parents.

Sowon also learned to respect her **elders.** When her family visited her Grandma Song at Christmas, she bowed before her grandmother with one knee on the ground. Her brother bowed with both knees on the ground. Then Sowon ran to her grandmother's Christmas tree to see her favorite ornament. It was a little girl with a blanket in her arms.

Sowon explains in her own words how she feels: "When I asked my mother if I could get my ears pierced, she said no. I begged, but I didn't talk back. I wouldn't do it. It's just the way we are. It's the way we live. We learn by example. If you respect other people, they'll respect you, too."

Respect—What Does It Mean?

**"I had never cared about acceptance
as much as I cared about respect."**
—Jackie Robinson

One day when I was in fifth grade, my teacher read some poems to us. The music and rhythm of the words marched in my head. When she finished reading, my teacher encouraged us to write our own poems. By this time, I was on fire. Eager to start, I grabbed my pencil, which flew across my paper as ideas popped like electricity in my mind. I wrote about an old Swiss watch that had always kept perfect time and then suddenly didn't. It was kind of a silly poem. I remember raising my hand several times to ask how to spell different words. My teacher grew more and more interested in what I was writing, and soon she was looking over my shoulder.

At the end of the writing period, she asked us to turn our papers in. My chest was bursting because I felt so proud of my poem. Then the bombshell hit. There, in front of the class with all my friends listening, the teacher took my paper, read through it quickly, and then looked at me with one eyebrow raised. "Where did this poem *really* come from?" she asked. "You must have memorized it and copied it from a book."

I felt crushed and embarrassed. I knew I was an honest person. I was proud of my poem, and her words stung me. At that moment I knew my teacher didn't **respect** me.

When you respect someone, you care about how the person feels. You believe that the person's ideas, thoughts, and feelings are important. You believe that he or she deserves to be treated kindly and politely.

My teacher embarrassed me. Embarrassing someone is **disrespectful**—it doesn't show respect. If the teacher thought I'd stolen the poem from somewhere else, she should have talked to me in private. I hadn't, and she didn't. I don't remember what I said to her—I only remember the hurt.

Maybe something like that has happened to you. It's okay. You can use it to learn to be stronger. I've never forgotten how that teacher treated me. Partly because of that, I'm a better teacher. I've always been careful to respect my own students and the things they write, say, and feel.

Respect is a special kind of caring. We can respect people we know well, and also people we don't know well at all. That's because part of respect is valuing people as human beings. Human beings deserve to be treated kindly and thoughtfully. You're a human being, so you deserve respect, too—from others, and from yourself.

How Can You Show Respect?

There are many ways you show respect. You show it by how you treat other people and yourself. That's right, part of respect is caring about *yourself.* You show it by caring about other living things, like animals and trees, and about the air and water living things need. You show it by following rules and laws. And you show it by paying attention to people's beliefs and customs.

Respect Yourself

You can't really respect others until you respect yourself. This means that you're nice to *you.* How? For starters, you don't say bad things about yourself or put yourself down.

Instead of saying, "I can't do it," you say, "I'll keep trying." Instead of thinking, "I'm not smart or popular," you think, "I'm good at lots of things, and I have friends who really like and trust me."

When you respect yourself, you care for your body and mind. You get a good night's sleep. You put your sweatshirt on when you go out in the wind. You eat healthy food and avoid too many sweets. You don't take drugs that your doctor didn't prescribe. You don't smoke cigarettes or drink alcohol. You wear a safety helmet when you ride a bike and a seat belt when you ride in a car. You don't take silly risks to pretend you are brave. It *isn't* brave to jump from the highest rock into a lake when you don't know what's under the water. Or to run across the street without looking for cars. Those are unsafe things to do.

It's important to respect your body, mind, feelings, and heart. If you don't respect yourself, how can anyone else?

**"How you carry yourself, what you stand for—
that's how you gain respect."**

—Mildred D. Taylor

Respect Other People

Remember to treat your family, friends, teachers, and other adults with respect. This means you let your mom sleep when she's been up late working. It means you sit down and play with your little brother for a while, even though you think his games are boring. It means you do the work your teacher assigns. It means you answer your grandpa when he talks to you. It means you listen to your friend when she's sad. Respecting others means you care about their feelings and the things they think are important.

You also show respect for others by the way you talk to them. It's good to keep in mind that your voice can sound mean even when your words don't. If you treat others with respect, they'll probably treat you with more respect, too. When you want to say something mean or sassy, zip your lips shut and count to ten. Think how the other person might feel if you let those words fly. Think how you might feel if someone said them to you.

"Think before you speak, and look before you leap."

—Irish proverb

Respect Differences

You can get in the habit of treating *all* people with respect. Lots of people are different from you in many ways. You may know people whose race, religion, skin color, or clothing is different from yours. *Different* doesn't mean *bad* or *wrong*.

   Respect the differences. Try to learn more about people who aren't like you. The ways we're different make us interesting!

Use Good Manners

Did anyone ever tell you to "Remember your manners"? Manners are another way people show respect. It's respectful to speak in a kind voice and use words like "Please," "Thank you," "Excuse me," and "May I?" Good manners mean you act kindly to others, too. Maybe you offer to help carry someone's books or groceries. Maybe you open a door for someone. You show good manners in the way you eat, dress, walk, and talk.

FIND OUT MORE . . .
Social Smarts: Modern Manners for Today's Kids by Elizabeth James (New York: Clarion Books, 1996). Advice on how to handle all kinds of social and personal situations. Ages 9–13.

Respect Property

Another part of respect is taking care of things that belong to you and other people. If you respect property, you don't write or draw on the school bathroom walls. You bring your toys and games in out of the rain so they won't be ruined. You're careful not to scratch cars that you pass on the street or in the garage, or walls and furniture at school, at the library, and at home (your home or someone else's). You put used paper in the recycling box. You take only what you need and what you'll use of everything.

Respect Nature and Other Living Things

You show respect for animals, plants, and nature by what you *do* and what you *don't* do. You *do* walk quietly past a nest of bird's eggs. You *don't* throw rocks or sticks at birds. You *do* take good care of the neighbors' hamster while they're away. You *don't* forget to clean the cage. You *do* put your gum wrapper in your pocket instead of dropping it on the ground. You *do* plant trees and water them. You *don't* peel the bark or snap off branches. You show respect for the earth all around you.

Respect Laws, Beliefs, and Customs

Following rules and laws is another way you show respect. This means you come inside from playing when your mom or dad tells you to. That's the rule. It means you don't shove in the halls at school. That's the rule. It means you don't throw rocks at windows. That's the law. It means you pay for the cool stuff you want from the store. That's the law, too.

You probably know many ways to be respectful about beliefs and customs. You can show respect for your country by standing and saying the "Pledge of Allegiance." You can show respect for your faith by learning its words, teachings, and prayers. (You can also show it by *not* talking, giggling, or laughing rudely in a place of worship.) You can show respect for other people's beliefs and customs by asking politely about them and not making fun of them.

FIND OUT MORE . . .

Kids of all ages will enjoy this recording of music from cultures all around the world: *A Child's Celebration of the World* (Music for Little People, Warner Brothers Records, 1998). Find it at a local library or store, or write to Music for Little People, P.O. Box 1460, Redway, CA 95560-1460. Toll-free phone: 1-800-346-4445. Email: musicforlittlepeople@mflp.com. Web site: *www.mflp.com.*

7 WAYS TO SHOW RESPECT

Reach out to others and learn about their beliefs and customs.

Enjoy the differences among people—they make life interesting!

Show respect for rules and laws by obeying them.

Put on your best manners. Speak politely, help people, and choose kind words.

Eat right, get plenty of sleep and exercise, learn healthy habits, and respect yourself.

Care about plants and animals and the air and water that living things need.

Treat property that belongs to you and other people carefully.

7 WAYS TO SPEAK UP WHEN YOU FEEL DISRESPECTED

Sometimes, even when you try your hardest to be kind, someone else might snap at you. It's okay to stick up for yourself. Here are some ways to do it:

Stay respectful even if you don't feel respected.

Plan what you're going to say—don't just say the first thing that comes into your head.

Earn respect by caring about everyone involved. Don't get rid of your hurt by hurting someone else.

Ask for the other side of the story. Get the facts straight.

Keep your comments short and clear.

Understand how the other person feels. Sometimes people say they're mad when they're really sad, jealous, hurt, or confused. Ask questions so you understand.

Practice good manners. Politely tell the person how you feel and what you need. Work together to find a solution.

FIND OUT MORE . . .

Stick Up For Yourself! Every Kid's Guide to Personal Power and Positive Self-Esteem (Revised and Updated Edition) by Gershen Kaufman, Ph.D., Lev Raphael, Ph.D., and Pamela Espeland (Minneapolis: Free Spirit Publishing, 1999). Simple words and real-life examples show you how you can stick up for yourself with other kids, big sisters and brothers, even grown-ups. Ages 8–12.

What If?

Here are some situations for you to think about, write about, talk about, or act out.

1. Your three-year-old brother goes into your drawer and throws your card collection all over the floor, chewing up and tearing some of the cards. What might you do to show respect to your brother *and* help him learn to have respect for your things?

2. You're walking by the bus stop, and your friend pulls out a bright red marker and starts drawing on the bench. She hands you another marker. What might happen if you try to stop your friend from drawing on the bench? If you don't? What might you do to show your friend you respect her and help her respect public property, too?

3. The sitter is rude to you and tells you to shut your mouth and stay in your room all day. Should you do anything to help the sitter show more respect for you? If so, what? If not, why? What might happen if you do something about it? If you don't?

More Ways to Show Respect

Here are some activities you can do to find more ways to be respectful.

Throw Disrespectful Words in the Garbage

Make a list of all the bad things you have said to yourself. Maybe you've called yourself "stupid," "ugly," or "clumsy." Write down all the disrespectful things you can remember saying or thinking. When you're done, take the list and tear it up. Crumple the scraps and throw them away. Promise yourself that you're *done* saying unkind things to yourself! Promise you won't do it again. You can do the same thing for unkind words you've said to other people.

Practice Good Table Manners

Manners are magic—people respect you more when you eat politely. To learn good table manners, hold a "good manners meal." Ask an adult to show you how to eat and speak politely at a meal. Look in a cookbook or the book below for instructions on how to set the table, pass dishes, eat, and talk during your meal. If you like, your meal could be a dessert party. Use plates, napkins, and silverware along with your cupcakes, ice cream, or other goodies. Keep practicing this yummy habit.

FIND OUT MORE . . .
Soup Should Be Seen and Not Heard: The Kid's Etiquette Book by Beth Brainard and Sheila Behr (New York: Dell, 1990). This book uses fun and humor to offer guidelines for using manners when you're eating, dressing, talking on the phone, and in other social situations. Ages 8 and up.

Make a Respect Mobile

Here's what you'll need:
- Drawing paper
- Scissors
- Crayons, colored pencils, or markers
- Hole punch
- Wire or plastic coat hanger
- String

Make a mobile to hang in your room, kitchen, club, or class. Cut sheets of drawing paper in half diagonally. On each half-sheet, draw a picture that shows something about respect. Make a small hole in the top of each piece and tie one end of a string to it. Tie the other ends of all the strings to the coat hanger. Hang your mobile in your room at home, the kitchen, or your classroom. If you like, use some of the following ideas of situations where people can show respect:

- talking with others
- walking and moving around
- playing or working with animals
- eating
- listening
- thinking about yourself
- noticing other people's customs
- following rules

REMINDER:
Don't forget to keep track of your progress on the "Building My Character Muscles" chart (page 16).

Make Family Respect Rules

As a family, talk about ways you can show respect to each other at home. What rules can you come up with that feel right to everyone? Make a "Respect in Our Family" chart and display it on a bulletin board or the refrigerator. You might want to include rules for parents, for kids, for sisters and brothers, for beliefs and customs, and for property. This is a nice activity for a family meeting. See "Have Family Meetings" (pages 37–38) to learn more about family meetings.

Read Stories About Respect

Altogether, One at a Time by E.L. Konigsburg (New York: Aladdin Paperbacks, 1989). A collection of four short stories about kids who learn to respect people whose race, age, body, or way of learning is different from their own. Ages 9–13.

Ella Enchanted by Gail Levine (New York: HarperCollins, 1997). Determined to be herself, Ella struggles to get rid of a childhood curse that makes her obey all orders without thinking. Based on the story of Cinderella. Ages 8–12.

The House of Wings by Betsy Byars (New York: Puffin Books, 1993). Left with his grandfather until his parents are settled in Detroit, Sammy learns to respect and love him. Ages 9–12.

It's a Spoon, Not a Shovel by Caralyn Buehner (New York: Dial Books for Young Readers, 1995). A mother tells her child, "It's a spoon, not a shovel," in this hilarious quiz on good manners. Ages 8 and up.

Richard Wright and the Library Card by William Miller (New York: Lee & Low Books, 1997). In the 1920s, Richard Wright cannot get a library card because he's black. With the help of a friend, he finds a way to use the library, which opens up the world of books to him. A true story about the meaning of respect and self-respect. Ages 6–9.

RESPONSIBILITY

Lawrence
Champagne III

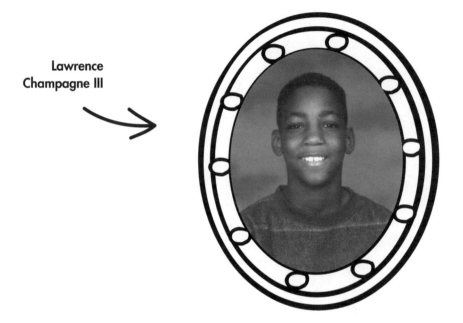

Someone Who's Responsible

Lawrence Champagne III and a Runaway Bus
St. Louis, Missouri

Lawrence (Larry) Champagne has always taken his responsibility to help other people seriously. His mom says, "He watches out for his brother and sister, and if I need anything, he helps me."

Larry helps his grandmother as well. He lifts heavy things and vacuums and scrubs floors for her. Then he hangs around his grandfather and watches him repair cars. "My grandpa taught me about driving and what to do in emergencies," Larry says. Luckily, he remembered it all, because when Larry was in the fifth grade, he took charge at a dangerous time.

Larry was peacefully sitting on the Mayflower Bus on his way to Bellerive Elementary School. His little brother sat next to him. The bus was filled with about twenty kids, ages five through ten. Larry was gazing straight ahead when he saw the bus driver's head fall to one side. The bus swerved out of control and hit the guardrail. The bus driver toppled out of her seat and landed on the boarding stairs. Larry sprung out of his seat. Kids screamed.

Larry hung onto the seats and fought his way to the front. The bus hit the guardrail again. Then a pick-up truck smashed into it, and Larry banged into a seat. Several kids toppled into the aisle. Still, the bus lurched forward. Larry pulled himself toward the front. He leaped behind the steering wheel. Stretching his foot down, he hit the brakes. The bus slammed to a stop, thrusting kids into the backs of seats. Larry and three other students tried to help the bus driver, who'd had a **stroke.** They opened the emergency exits so the frightened children could leave. Five students were injured, but because of Larry's fast action, no one was killed.

A **stroke** is a sudden loss of blood to the brain.

Larry doesn't think he did anything special. "I just did what had to be done," he explains.

His mom says, "Larry's a responsible kid. He's always putting others before himself. Now he wants to install a motion detector light outside our house. I don't think he knows much about electricity," she laughs, "but he promised to find an electrician to teach him. You can count on Larry. That's the way he is."

Responsibility—
What Does It Mean?

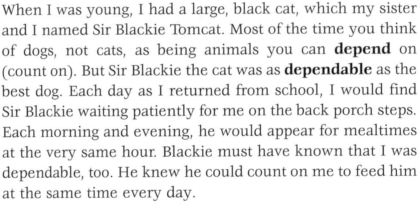

*"I learned the value of hard work and
persistence from my family."*
—*Michael Jordan*

When I was young, I had a large, black cat, which my sister
and I named Sir Blackie Tomcat. Most of the time you think
of dogs, not cats, as being animals you can **depend** on
(count on). But Sir Blackie the cat was as **dependable** as the
best dog. Each day as I returned from school, I would find
Sir Blackie waiting patiently for me on the back porch steps.
Each morning and evening, he would appear for mealtimes
at the very same hour. Blackie must have known that I was
dependable, too. He knew he could count on me to feed him
at the same time every day.

One day, when the two of us were on the porch, a big
angry dog came down our driveway, snarling at Sir Blackie.
It was well known that this dog ate cats for dessert. I jumped
up, yelling at the dog and waving him away. Sir Blackie
never moved from his perch on the porch. He just kept
purring. He must have known that he could depend on me
again. And he was right. I shooed that mean dog away.

I was **responsible** for Blackie, and he must have known he
could always depend on me to care for him and keep him safe.

You need to be responsible, too. A responsible person
does what he or she promises to do. In that way, it's like
being trustworthy. Your mom needs to know that if you tell
her you'll be home at a certain time, you'll be there. If you
run into a problem, you'll call her on the phone. When

people know that you're responsible, they don't have to worry so much about you. Parents will usually give you more freedom, and teachers will usually give you more privileges. **Responsibility** helps you learn to be a leader—someone who starts things and keeps them going. It means taking responsibility for *yourself,* too—learning to think about choices and make good decisions about ways to act and things to do. Being responsible helps make the world a better place.

How Can You Be Responsible?

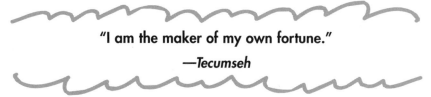

"I am the maker of my own fortune."

—Tecumseh

Each of us is responsible for our own actions, words, thoughts, and choices. What does this mean for you?

Your Actions

You're responsible for the good things you choose to do. Do you hand in your homework on time? Do you complete your chores at home when they need to be done? Do you take care of your own clothes or toys? Do you keep yourself healthy by eating good foods? Do you try to keep yourself safe? Do you follow rules at home and at school? Do you obey laws in your community? If you do, you're being responsible.

You also choose the way you treat the environment around you. Do you take care not to litter? Do you stop others from littering? Do you recycle paper, cans, or old socks? Do you treat animals with kindness? If you have a pet, do you feed and care for it?

Are you responsible about property? Do you vacuum carefully so you don't bang walls and furniture? Do you handle the dishes carefully when you wash them? Do you put away your books and papers so you can find them easily?

Your Words

Being responsible for your words means that when you *say* you'll do something, you follow up and *do* it. You don't make promises you can't keep. It also means that you think before you speak. You control the words that fly out of your mouth, and you can decide to say something or nothing. You can choose to use kind words or unkind words. You *can't* control the things other people say to you, but you *can* control the things you say back.

Your Thoughts

You're also responsible for the things you think about. "But wait!" you might say. "Ideas pop into my head all the time. Sometimes the ideas that come are bad ones. I can't control that." This might be true. Still, you *can* decide whether to let a bad idea stay in your mind. What can you do to get rid of it? Try ignoring it. Think about something good instead. Or change your activity. You can switch the TV channel or pick up a good book and read. You can talk to a friend or play a game with your brother or sister. Good things crowd out bad things.

> ## IMPORTANT!
> Sometimes people have so many bad thoughts they don't know what to do. If this happens to you, talk to an adult you trust. Tell the person about the thoughts that won't go away. When you find you can't change something by yourself, the responsible thing to do is get help.

Making Choices

Here's a story about making choices:

Seth, a fourth-grade boy, chose not to go straight home after school one day. A friend convinced him to stop at the grocery store to buy some soda pop. Seth thought, "It's okay. I'll only be a few minutes late."

At the store, Seth watched as his friend stuffed gum and candy bars into his coat pockets. Then he stuffed some candy into Seth's pocket. Seth started to pull the candy out, but his friend stopped him. "Don't worry," the friend said. "You won't be taking it. You didn't put the candy in your pocket—I did. So you're okay."

Seth thought, "That's right. I didn't take the candy. It's not my fault." Seth wanted to please his friend.

The boys went to leave the store. At the door, a man with a gold "Manager" label on his shirt stopped them. The store's security cameras had caught the boys stealing. Seth tried to explain that he wasn't the one stealing, but the manager didn't believe him. The police didn't either. Seth was sent to juvenile court—a court for young people. He now had a juvenile record with the police, and he had to complete twenty-five hours of community service. Seth learned the hard way that he'd better think about **consequences**—about what might happen—*before* he makes a choice.

Where do you think Seth made his first poor choice? If you answer, "When he didn't go home after school," you're right. Seth's second poor choice was staying and watching his friend steal. His third was allowing his friend to put stolen candy in his own pocket.

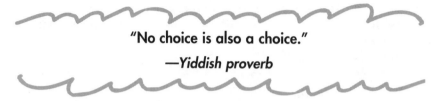

"No choice is also a choice."
—Yiddish proverb

It's not always easy to make the right choice. But making good choices is part of being responsible. Here are three steps that can help you make better choices:

1. Think before you act. Before you decide to do something, think about what might happen next. Seth could have done this at any point along the way—and stayed out of trouble. He might have thought: "Why is my friend going to the store? What does he need me for? Should I call my mom first? If I don't go straight home, she'll worry about me. She might get mad. She might ground me. Maybe she won't trust me anymore . . . What if I get hurt? No one will know where I am, so no one will come to help me . . . Why is my friend putting candy in his pocket? Maybe he's stealing it . . . What if I leave the store with candy in my pocket? What if someone sees me? Will I get in trouble? Will I feel guilty? Will I respect myself? Will other people respect me?"

2. Gather the facts. There are always facts to think about. Seth might have asked: "Where's the store? How long will it take to get there? How long will it take me to walk home from there? Could I check with Mom first? What other choices do I have?" This last question can help you sort out an important fact—the choice itself. Ask yourself, "What are my choices?"

3. Decide which choice is best for *you* and the right thing to do. Seth had lots of choices. He chose to go with his friend, but he could have said no. He could have called home first. Maybe he could have asked the friend home instead. Seth wanted to please his friend, though. Because of that, Seth forgot to be responsible to *himself.* The best choice isn't always the easiest one. Still, Seth would have been better off if he'd thought, "My friend might think I'm stupid if I call my mom first, but it will be better for me if I do."

IMPORTANT!
Even though you can help other people, you are *not* responsible for things that other people say and do. And when there's no choice, you're not responsible. If an adult or someone bigger than you forces you to do something that doesn't feel right to you, you have no choice. Think about a different grown-up who can help. Talk to your dad, mom, another relative, your teacher, the school counselor, or your club, scout, or church leader.

Making good choices can help you feel better about yourself and your life. You'll be happier and healthier. You'll have friends who care about you. Your family, teachers, and other people will trust you.

3 STEPS IN MAKING GOOD CHOICES

1. Think *before* you act.

2. Gather the facts.

3. Decide which choice is best for *you* and the right thing to do.

Getting Organized

Suppose you know that you're supposed to stop by your piano teacher's after school, pick up some bread at the corner store, read a story, and feed the cat. You'll probably try to do all of those things. But many kids don't complete tasks—not because they don't want to do them but because they *forget.* They need to get organized and make a plan.

How do you make a plan? Follow these steps:

1. Write a list of all the things you need to do. (Your list might be a plan for the day, for the week, or for the weekend.) Write all the things you can think of. Then put a "1" by the most important thing. Put a "2" by the next most important thing, and so on. This will help you keep in mind what you *most* need to do. If you only finish part of the things on your list, at least you'll get the most important ones done.

2. Write down when each task needs to be done. If you're planning the day, does it need to be done before breakfast? After school? If you're planning the week, does it need to be done Wednesday? Before Friday night? Maybe your dad wants you to wash the kitchen floor by Saturday afternoon. You can do it earlier if you want.

3. Write down the things you'll need to do each job. If you have to draw a map for school, you might need a pencil, an eraser, markers, paper, and a ruler. But maybe you don't have markers. So if you write down what you need, you can remember to ask your dad or mom to help you get them.

4. Make a backup plan. You need to know ahead what you can do if your first idea doesn't work. What if you wait until Saturday morning to clean the kitchen floor and your grandma is in there making pickles? If you have a backup plan, you'll think ahead about this and maybe wash the floor on Friday afternoon after school.

HOW TO PLAN

1. Write a list of all the things you need to do.

2. Write down when each task needs to be done.

3. Write down the things you'll need to do each job.

4. Make a backup plan.

Here's an example of a plan you might write for yourself:

Number the items, starting with "1" for what's most important	**Job or task**	**Done by when?**	**What I need so I can do it**	**Backup plan**
3.	Wash kitchen floor	Saturday afternoon (do that morning)	Bucket, mop, vinegar, clean rags	Ask when Nana needs the kitchen. If Saturday morning won't work, do Friday after school.
1.	Read two chapters	Thursday morning (read Monday night)	Remember to bring home that book!	Read Tuesday night if Monday's game runs late.
2.	Scoop out kitty litter	Monday, Wednesday, Friday (do before school)	Scoop, fresh litter	Do right after school if no time in morning.

6 WAYS TO MAKE RESPONSIBLE CHOICES

Consider what might happen—think before you act.

Help yourself be responsible by getting and staying organized.

Obey rules and laws in your home, school, and community.

Ignore bad ideas that pop into your head. Change what you're doing or think about something good instead.

Choose the choice that's best for you and for others—the one that feels right inside.

Earn people's trust by showing that they can count on you.

What If?

Here are some situations for you to think about, write about, talk about, or act out.

1. It's your turn to set the table, but you also have two pages of math to do. It's late, and you don't think you have time to do both. Should you ask your little brother to set the table so you can do your math? Should you set the table and forget your math? How would you handle this and be responsible?

2. Your teacher asks you to get a book from the public library to bring to class tomorrow. You say you will, but when you get home, your parents are too busy to drive you to the library. You get angry because you think your parents are making you look like you're not responsible—you don't have the book, and you've become upset. What might be the responsible thing for you to do? How might you avoid having the same problem again?

3. You're walking to a band concert where you're going to play the French horn. It takes about twenty minutes to get from your home to the school. When you're halfway there, you realize that you forgot your music. You promised you'd be on time for the practice before the concert, but you need your music, too. The practice begins in ten minutes. What would be the responsible thing to do?

More Ways to Be Responsible

Here are some activities you can do to find more ways to be responsible.

Make a "Who's Responsible?" Chart

Here's what you'll need:
- Chart paper
- Marker
- Self-stick notes

Make a chart of tasks or jobs that need to be done at home. Maybe you'll make a chores chart. Maybe you'll chart who'll do what to get ready for a camping trip or to complete a family project. Across the top, make three columns and write "What?," "Who?," and "Done." On the left side of the chart paper, list the tasks that need to be completed. You can write the family names on self-stick notes and stick them in the spaces to show who'll do which jobs. After finishing a job, the person can move the note with his or her name on it to the "Done" column.

For more ideas on planning choices, see "Make a Cooperative Chores Chart" (page 51) and "Make Family Chores Fair" (pages 61–62).

Make a Choices Log

Here's what you'll need:

- Notebook and pen or pencil
- *If you wish:* Materials for decorating your notebook (such as paints, markers, colored pencils, pictures cut from magazines, glue stick, ribbon, and stickers)

A log is a kid of list, diary, or journal. When you write in it, you tell the date and describe something that happened. Make a "Choices Log" to keep track of times when you made choices you felt good or not-so-good about. (*Examples:* Maybe you chose a healthy snack instead of a candy bar. Maybe you chose to break a rule during a game at school.) For each entry, think about these questions:

- What happened?
- Did you make the right choice? Explain.
- If you *did* make the right choice, was it hard or easy? Why? If you *didn't,* why did you choose as you did?
- How did you feel about the choice you made? How do you feel about it now?
- What did you learn that will help you in the future?

Make Your Own Daily Planning Calendar

Here's what you'll need:

- Three-ring notebook or cardboard binder with metal fasteners
- Label and marker
- 12 copies of "My Daily Plan" on page 135 (*Hint:* Copy the form at 110% for the best fit in your three-ring notebook.)
- Hole punch
- Pencil and eraser

- *If you wish:* Materials to decorate the notebook or binder (such as markers, ribbon, glitter glue, buttons, and other items)

1. On the copies of the form, write the name of each month in the space provided. Then number the days from the first day of the month. (Your parent, older brother or sister, or teacher can help you do this.)

2. Put the forms inside the folder or binder. Use a marker to label the outside of the planning calendar.

3. Start with the present month and write the homework, lessons, sports, chores, or other activities you will do each day. Write in pencil so you can erase if something changes.

Make a habit of checking your calendar each day and checking off, adding, or changing items so you'll always be up to date.

Volunteer with Your Club or Family

One of the best ways to help others is by volunteering to do a job once a week or once a month. This is a great chance to do something with a club or group you're in, or with your family. There are lots of things you could do. How about reading to younger kids for story hour at the library? Serving ice cream or helping with games at a health care center? Handing out or collecting programs for a religious service? To find out how to get started, check with the organization where you want to help (such as the library, senior center, or place of worship). Local newspapers often list volunteer opportunities, too.

When you agree to volunteer on a regular schedule, it's important to go every time and be on time. If you're sick or can't go, call ahead so another volunteer can be found.

REMINDER: Don't forget to keep track of your progress on the "Building My Character Muscles" chart (page 16).

Read Stories About Responsibility

Earthquake Terror by Peg Kehret (New York: Puffin Books, 1996). When twelve-year-old Jonathan goes camping in northern California, an earthquake hits. Jonathan must find a way to keep his partially paralyzed younger sister, himself, and the dog alive until help arrives. Ages 8–12.

If You Had to Choose, What Would You Do? by Sandra McLeod Humphrey (Amherst, NY: Prometheus Books, 1995). A good book for figuring out how to make responsible choices. Ages 4–8.

Jamaica's Find by Juanita Havill (Boston: Houghton Mifflin, 1986). Jamaica finds a stuffed dog on the playground and has to decide whether to seek out the owner or keep it. Ages 4–8.

A Promise Is a Promise by Robert Munsch and Michael Kusugak (Buffalo, NY: Firefly Books, 1988). An Inuit child learns the meaning of the words "A promise is a promise" after she encounters imaginary Arctic creatures under the ice. Ages 4–8.

Titanic Crossing by Barbara Williams (New York: Dial Books for Young Readers, 1995). When the *Titanic* hits an iceberg, Albert knows that his first responsibility is to his little sister. He risks his own life to save hers. Ages 8–12.

"For those who are willing to make an effort, great miracles and wonderful treasures are in store."

—Isaac Bashevis Singer

My Daily Plan

Month _____ Year _____

Sunday	Monday	Tuesday	Wednesday	Thursday	Friday	Saturday

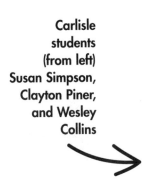

Carlisle students (from left) Susan Simpson, Clayton Piner, and Wesley Collins

SAFETY

Kids Who Work for Safety

Students at Carlisle School
Covington, Kentucky

Third and fourth graders at Carlisle School in Covington, Kentucky, banged their fists on their desks. They were angry. Three little kids had been hit by cars in front of their school and rushed to hospitals. The brother of one of the kids had been hit by a car that jumped the curb and dragged him into the street.

"This is totally insane," Clayton complained. "Now it seems like the cars are coming after us."

"This happens all the time," Brandy added.

Ms. Joan Behnke, their teacher, had trained her students to solve problems in their neighborhood, so the kids were quick to notice problems that needed attention. She listened and said, "What do you want to do about it? You're the Community Problem Solving Team. You should think of some solutions."

"Let's call the police," Susan suggested, "and find out how many kids have been hit."

That's what Susan did. She called the police. They said that 235 kids had been hit coming or going from Covington schools in the last four years. And that was just the number of kids who'd gone to hospitals.

Rodney said, "That doesn't count the kids who got hit but didn't have to go to the hospital."

"If you don't learn to be safe," said Brittany, "no one will do it for you."

The kids put their heads together. They decided it was up to them to teach young kids how to be street-smart. So they created a skit to teach children how to play it safe. They wore mouse costumes and used music to make the skit interesting and fun.

But that wasn't enough for the Community Problem Solving Team. They made a video of their skit to loan out to others, and they held a poster contest. They also invited someone from Project Safe Place to speak to their school. Through Project Safe Place, the team learned how to set up programs to give kids safe places to go for help, and what to do in order to be safe.

With all this flurry of work, the kids won an award in the International Community Problem Solving contest. But there was an even better reward.

"After that," smiled Wesley, holding up his thumb, "not *one* child at Carlisle School was hit by a car all year!"

FIND OUT MORE . . .

To learn how to start a problem solving program in your school or community, contact this organization:

Future Problem Solving Program
Community Problem Solving
2500 Packard Road, Suite 110
Ann Arbor, MI 48104-6827
Toll-free phone: 1-800-256-1499
Web site: *www.fpsp.org*

Safety—What Does It Mean?

"The world's children deserve to walk the earth in safety."
—*Bill Clinton, 42nd U.S. president*

One day ten-year-old Teng was swimming at the city pool with some friends. It was a hot afternoon, and the pool was crowded. Teng watched as a little boy ran, laughing, near the edge of the pool. Suddenly the boy slipped and tumbled into the water. "Help!" the boy shrieked as his head went under. His arms and legs splashed every which way.

Teng thought and acted quickly. First, he grabbed a safety ring from the side of the pool and threw it to the boy.

At the same time, Teng yelled to a man sitting nearby, "That boy fell in! He needs help!" Then Teng hurried to get the lifeguard. By the time the lifeguard dove in and swam toward the boy, the man had pulled the child out of the pool to safety. Thanks to Teng's quick, safe actions, the little boy didn't drown.

When you think about being **safe,** what comes to mind? Swimming with a buddy and where there's a lifeguard? Crossing streets carefully? Using a helmet when you ride a bike and a seat belt when you're in a car?

The National Safety Council says that in 1997 more than 1,000 children ages fourteen and under drowned. In 1996 more than 35,700 people were hurt on skateboards and treated in the hospital. In the same year, over 566,000 people were rushed to the hospital with bicycle injuries. That's a lot of hurt people. This gives you a good idea why knowing about **safety** can help to protect you.

Safety means being free from harm or risk. To be safe, you need to be careful. At home, some ways to be safe are keeping the door locked, staying away from the stove or fireplace, and not playing with matches. Safety at school includes walking in the halls instead of running, and using safety equipment for science and gym. Out on your own, you keep safe by staying close to your home or neighborhood and not talking to strangers.

Part of being safe is *feeling* safe inside. "But," you might say, "lots of bad things happen. I can't stop all of them. So how can I feel safe inside?"

It's true that you can't stop all bad things from happening. But you can learn and follow safety guidelines. You can learn what you need to be careful about. Knowing what to do and being careful can help you be safe *and* feel safer inside.

How Can You Be Safe?

There are three important things you can do to help yourself be safe:

- Know the safety rules and guidelines to follow at school, at home, in activities, and on your own.
- Know what to do in an emergency.
- Make good choices when you're in an unsafe or tricky situation.

Know Safety Rules

Do you know the safety guidelines about letting people into your house or apartment building? About using the toaster, stove, microwave, washer, or dryer in your home? Do you know the safety rules for the bus you ride to school? The pool where you swim? The playground where you shoot baskets? The ice rink where you figure skate or play hockey?

Most places and activities have rules you can follow to be safe. If you're not sure what they are, ask an adult who's in charge to point out the rules and explain them.

FIND OUT MORE . . .

The National Safety Council has all kinds of statistics. If you visit the Web site, you can get a copy of "The Safe-T Rangers on Vacation," a fun story about seat-belt safety with activity pages:

National Safety Council
1121 Spring Lake Drive
Itasca, IL 60143-3201
Toll-free phone: 1-800-621-7615
Web site: *www.nsc.org/*
Web site link for "Safe-T Rangers": *www.nsc.org/traf/sbc/safet.htm*

Write or call the Bicycle Helmet Safety Institute for ideas on buying helmets, statistics, and more (remember to ask permission before making a long-distance phone call):

Bicycle Helmet Safety Institute
4611 Seventh Street South
Arlington, VA 22204-1419
Phone number: (703) 486-0100
Web site: *www.helmets.org*

Know What to Do in an Emergency

An **emergency** is a dangerous situation that needs to be helped right away. In an emergency, quick thinking can keep you and everyone else safe. For any emergency, it's important to stay calm, think, and act quickly.

Talk to your dad, mom, or guardian about emergencies that might happen at home and what you should do if one *does* happen. What if a pan catches fire on the stove? If your little sister swallows a toy? If your older brother falls and hits his head? Talk with your teacher, coach, or club leader, too. Ask what you should do when emergencies happen during school or other activities.

6 STEPS TO TAKE IN AN EMERGENCY

1. Stay calm.

2. Find a grown-up who can help right away.

3. If you can't find a trusted adult, call "9-1-1" or dial "0" for the operator.

4. Tell the problem to the person on the phone. Tell it as clearly and briefly as you can.

5. Tell the person your full name and the address or place you're calling from.

6. Stay on the phone to answer and ask questions and to get more instructions.

FIND OUT MORE . . .

Here are some resources about dealing with emergencies:

KidsHealth.org for Kids is a Web site you can visit to learn about emergency first aid and safety around the house and out-doors. Go to: *www.kidshealth.org/kid/watch.*

Kids to the Rescue: First Aid Techniques for Kids by Maribeth and Darwin Boelts (Seattle, WA: Parenting Press, 1992). This book shows how to help out in fourteen different medical emergencies. Ages 7–12.

Now I Know Better: Kids Tell Kids About Safety by the Pediatric Emergency Department, Children's Hospital at Yale-New Haven (Brookfield, CT: Millbrook Press, 1996). Kids' own essays about accidents and emergencies they've experienced and what they've learned. Ages 9–12.

Make Safe Choices

To make good choices, it's important to keep yourself healthy. You might wonder, "What does being healthy have to do with making safe choices?" When you eat food that's good for you and get plenty of sleep and exercise, you feel

your best. Both your body and your mind are stronger. A strong body helps keep you safe from illness. A strong mind helps you think more clearly and make better choices.

What kinds of choices? There are lots of times when you can choose to do the safe thing. At school, it's a safe choice to decide not to be a bully, or not to hit back when someone *else* is a bully. On the way to and from school, it's a safe choice to walk in a group, cross at crosswalks, and stay away from strangers or gangs. If you see someone stealing something or hurting someone, it's a safe choice to tell an adult about it as soon as you can. Alone or with friends, it's a safe choice never to fool around with alcohol or other drugs. At home, it's a safe choice never to touch matches unless you're with an adult. In your home or someone else's, it's a safe choice *never* to play with—or even touch—a gun.

FIND OUT MORE . . .

Here are four books about making good choices:

Bullies Are a Pain in the Brain by Trevor Romain (Minneapolis: Free Spirit Publishing, 1997). A funny and helpful book to help you become "Bully-Proof." Ages 8–12.

Guns: What You Should Know by Rachel Schulson (Morton Grove, IL: Albert Whitman & Co., 1997). With all the shooting in movies and on TV, it can be hard to remember that guns can really hurt people. This book gives good information about guns and gun safety. Ages 4–8.

The Safe Zone: A Kid's Guide to Personal Safety by Donna Chaiet and Francine Russell (New York: William Morrow & Co., 1998). Teaches ideas for nonviolent self-defense. Includes lots of realistic "what if" situations. Ages 9–12.

What Would You Do? A Kid's Guide to Tricky and Sticky Situations by Linda Schwartz (Santa Barbara, CA: The Learning Works, 1990). A book that tells kids how to handle more than seventy situations from being locked out, lost, or followed to dealing with bullies, guns, drugs, and drunk adults. Ages 8–12.

Another important choice has to do with shows, movies, and games you see and play on TV and the computer. Watching **violence** and playing **violent** games won't help you feel safe and careful. Instead, it can make *you* feel violent, too. Violence is about hurting people. Hurting somebody isn't a safe thing to do. There are many other games and shows to play and watch. You can probably think of lots of safe, fun ways to play *without* violence.

" . . . the most important lesson for every time of life, is this: 'Never hurt anybody.'"

—*Denis Breeze*

Do you have a little voice inside you that sometimes tells you something doesn't feel safe? That little voice is called **instinct,** or a "gut feeling." Sometimes you just feel that things aren't right. Even if you can't say for sure what's wrong, it's usually a good choice to trust your instinct. Maybe you don't feel comfortable at a friend's home. Maybe you think a stranger is looking at you funny. You might wonder if you're just imagining things. But if something doesn't feel right to you, the best choice is to find a way to feel safe.

How? If you want to go home, call a parent or another adult you trust to come get you. If you're worried about a stranger, run home or run to a group of people. Or run to a safe house in your neighborhood.

In many communities there are safe places especially for kids who are bullied, followed, or hurt while walking in a neighborhood. One such place is a McGruff house. A McGruff house will have a picture of McGruff the Crime Dog with the words "McGruff house" in the window or on the door. Find out if there's a safe house or block-parent program in your neighborhood. Learn where it is. If

your neighborhood doesn't have one, tell your parents. Ask if they can work with your neighbors or police department to start one.

FIND OUT MORE . . .

Here's a group you can contact to find out how to start a McGruff program in your community. (Don't forget to ask permission before calling long distance.)

National Crime Prevention Council (NCPC)
1700 K Street, NW, 2nd Floor
Washington, DC 20006-3817
Phone number: (202) 466-6272
Web site: *www.ncpc.org/*

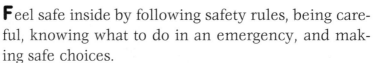

6 GUIDELINES FOR FEELING AND BEING SAFE

Stick to safety rules at school, on the bus, on the street, at home, and in sports and other activities. Stay away from dangerous things like drugs, alcohol, cigarettes, matches, fireworks, knives, and guns. Never touch any of these things if an adult isn't there.

Ask a trusted adult to help you if you see something dangerous or if you don't feel safe.

Feel safe inside by following safety rules, being careful, knowing what to do in an emergency, and making safe choices.

Encourage your friends to be safe, too. Stick to what you know is right even if friends tease you or try to change your mind.

Trust your instinct. Listen to the voice inside you that says something isn't right.

Yell for help if you're in danger.

> **IMPORTANT!**
>
> Maybe you don't feel safe at home or at school. Maybe a child or an adult you know is hurting you. Maybe you're afraid of bullies, or gangs, or guns in your neighborhood. Think about an adult you trust who can help you. This might be a parent, relative, neighbor, sitter, teacher, coach, group leader, or someone at your place of worship. Tell the person why you don't feel safe and ask for his or her help.

What If?

Here are some situations for you to think about, write about, talk about, or act out.

1. You have a friend who likes to play violent video games. He makes fun of you when you say you don't want to play. Other kids like your friend and listen to what your friend says. One day you're at your friend's home with a bunch of other kids. Everyone's taking turns with a violent game and teasing you to join in. The kids start shoving and punching. What can you do to keep yourself safe and to encourage your friends to be safe, too?

2. Your older sister takes you to her secret hideout. She makes you promise never to tell anyone about it. Her hide-out is a beautiful group of trees with a pond in the middle. Your sister says, "Come on in. The water's nice and warm in this pond." You know that swimming without adults is dangerous and that it's against your family's safety rules. But you want very much to have fun with your sister, and she is a good swimmer. How can you help both of you stay safe and still have her trust you?

3. You've been to a birthday party. Your friend's mother offers to drive all of you home. To save time, she starts loading all ten kids into one minivan. There aren't enough seat belts for each kid. You want to be respectful and polite to the mother, but you know what she's doing isn't safe. Is it possible to be polite and still stay safe? Why or why not? What can you do to be safe yourself? To help the other kids be safe?

More Ways to Be Safe

Here are some activities you can do to find more ways to help yourself and others be safe.

Make an Emergency Phone Number List

Here's what you'll need:

- Copies of "Emergency Phone Numbers" on page 150
- Phone book

Copy the "Emergency Phone Numbers" page and fill it in with your family. When you're done, display the list where you can see it easily while using the phone. This is a good activity for a family meeting (see "Have Family Meetings" on pages 37–38).

Do a Home Safety Check

Here's what you'll need:

- Copy of "Home Safety Checklist" on page 151

This is another good activity for a family meeting. With your family, check your house or apartment to see that it's as safe as possible. Make a copy of the "Home Safety Checklist." Walk through your home and check each item on the list. When you're done, figure out how the family can fix anything you found that wasn't safe.

Make a Safety Flyer

Here's what you'll need:
- Paper
- Pens, colored pencils, or fine-point markers

Make a safety flyer and pass it out in your school or neighborhood. You can use one of these ideas, or come up with one of your own:

- water safety
- walking safety
- bike safety
- fire safety
- bus safety

Water Safety Tips

* Learn how to swim.
* Never swim alone.
* Never swim in polluted water.
* Walk (don't run) around swimming pools.
* Make sure there's a lifeguard.
* Always wear a life jacket when boating or waterskiing.
* Don't play in fast-running streams or rivers.
* Don't play near water during a thunderstorm.
* Never walk or skate on frozen lakes, ponds, or streams unless you're at an open public rink or with an adult.

Plan to Be Safe During a Disaster

Here's what you'll need:
- Copy of "Let's Be Ready!" on page 152

A **disaster** is something dangerous that happens suddenly and affects people in a big way. Earthquakes, tornadoes, hurricanes, and fires are examples of disasters. With

REMINDER:
Don't forget to keep track of your progress on the "Building My Character Muscles" chart (page 16).

your family, class, or after-school group, talk about the types of disasters that could happen in your area. Make a copy of "Let's Be Ready!" and look together for the answers to the questions. Where can you go to get the information you need? You might:

- call a newspaper or TV station (or visit their Web site) to learn what to do in a weather emergency.
- find out where to call by checking the phone book under "Public Safety."
- call the local police or fire department (call the regular number, not "9-1-1" or another emergency number).

When you've finished filling out "Let's Be Ready!" display the sheet where everyone can see it easily, like on the refrigerator or bulletin board.

FIND OUT MORE . . .

Check out some of these books on dealing with disasters:

I'll Know What to Do: A Kid's Guide to Natural Disasters by Bonnie S. Mark and Aviva Layton (Washington, DC: Magination, 1997). Gives important tips on safety as well as ideas for understanding and handling fear and other feelings that come with disasters. Ages 8–13.

Fire Night! by Monica Driscoll Beatty (Santa Fe, NM: Health Press, 1999). Twelve-year-old Katy tells what she's learned about fire safety to overcome her fears and make the right decisions during a fire. Ages 4–8.

Tornado Alert by Giuilio Maestro and Franklyn Mansfield Branley (New York: HarperTrophy, 1990). Learn where, when, and how a tornado develops along with ways to keep safe when a tornado is near. Ages 4–8.

We Shake in a Quake by Hannah Gelman Givon (Berkeley, CA: Tricycle Press, 1996). Tips on what to do before, during, and after an earthquake. Ages 4–8.

Read Stories About Safety

The Boxcar Children by Gertrude Warner (Cutchogue, NY: Buccaneer Books, 1992). Four orphans who have run away from the grandfather they have never met make their home in an old railroad boxcar. Ages 8–10.

Dana Doesn't Like Guns Anymore by Carole Webb Moore-Slater (New York: Friendship Press, 1992). Dana learns that guns are dangerous when he plays with a friend's BB gun. Ages 7–10.

Officer Buckle and Gloria by Peggy Rathmann (New York: Putnam Publishing, 1995). Officer Buckle puts everyone to sleep with his dull lectures on safety, but his police dog, Gloria, knows how to liven things up. Ages 4–8.

Pedal Power by Judy Delton (New York: Yearling Books, 1998). A group of kids are planning a bike hike, but Roger thinks the safety rules are dumb. Ages 6–9.

Stolen Ponies by Jeanne Betancourt (New York: Little Apple, 1999). The "Pony Pals" discover that Tommy and Mike have been lighting campfires in the woods. Ages 9–12.

Emergency Phone Numbers

Who or what	Phone number
Local emergency number	_____
Fire department	_____
Police	_____
Poison control	_____
Disaster hotline	_____
Abuse hotline	_____
Doctor	_____
Ambulance	_____
Mom's/Dad's/ Guardian's work number	_____
Other relative or friend:	
_____	_____
Neighbor:	
_____	_____
Weather alert	_____
Power company	_____
Veterinarian	_____
Other numbers:	_____
_____	_____
_____	_____
_____	_____

Our phone number(s): _____

Our address: _____

Home Safety Checklist

Please check for dangers in your home. Make changes for each item checked "No."

Yes **No**

_____ _____ There are smoke detectors in bedrooms, kitchen, furnace room.

_____ _____ There are fire extinguishers on each floor and by the cooktop.

_____ _____ There are carbon monoxide detectors on each floor.

_____ _____ There are no electrical cords under rugs.

_____ _____ Wall plugs are not overloaded with many cords plugged in.

_____ _____ Paints, thinners, turpentine, and other flammable things are in closed, airtight containers.

_____ _____ Matches and lighters are safely stored out of reach of small children.

_____ _____ There are *no* oily, greasy rags lying around. These are placed in cans or jars with lids.

_____ _____ Pesticides and herbicides are in child- and animal-proof containers.

_____ _____ Cleaning fluids are out of reach of small children.

_____ _____ Guns are unloaded and are locked. Only adults have keys to gun storage cabinet.

_____ _____ Ammunition is stored separately. Only adults have access to key.

_____ _____ Fireworks are safely stored under lock and key. Only adults have access to key.

_____ _____ Furnaces and water heaters are checked each year.

_____ _____ Furnaces and water heaters are strapped down so that they cannot move around.

_____ _____ Medicines are out of reach of small children.

_____ _____ Medicines are stored in childproof containers.

_____ _____ Rugs are fastened down tightly.

_____ _____ All outside doors have deadbolts.

_____ _____ Windows can be locked shut.

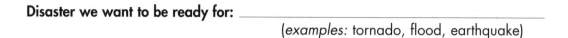

Disaster we want to be ready for: _____

(*examples:* tornado, flood, earthquake)

How will we know it is happening or will happen?
(*examples:* siren will sound, message will come on TV or radio)

Where should we go to be safe? What should we do there?
(*examples:* meet in cellar, gather on sidewalk in front of building)

What food or supplies should we have on hand?
(*examples:* water, cereal, radio, flashlight)

How will we know the disaster is over?
(*examples:* radio will say, "all clear" signal will sound)

What should we do to be safe after the disaster?
(*examples:* stay away from downed power lines, wait for parent before returning home)

DO's and DON'Ts during this disaster:
(*examples:* DO go to the hallway, DON'T stand near windows)

Glossary

adobe: made of clay or sun-dried earth

ancestors: relatives who lived before and are now gone, such as great-grandparents and great-great-grandparents

bilingual: using two different languages, like English and Vietnamese

caring: showing that you care about someone; showing concern, being kind, sharing, helping, and giving are all ways that you show you care

chairperson: a person in charge of a meeting

character: having positive qualities such as caring, fairness, honesty, respect, and responsibility

character trait: a certain positive quality that shows strong character

citizen: a person who lives in a community, state, province, or country; in a democracy, citizens have both freedoms (rights) and responsibilities

citizenship: being a member of a community, state, province, or country; the way you act as a member of a community

collage: a poster with lots of different pictures and words on it

conflict: a disagreement about a problem

consequence: what might happen as a result of something you do or say

cooperate: to work and play together peacefully; to work together on a job or on a problem that needs to be solved

cooperation: working or playing together peacefully

Creator: God; a Higher Power

democracy: a form of government where people choose their leaders by voting

depend: to count on

dependable: able to be counted on

disaster: something dangerous that happens suddenly and affects people in a big way

disrespectful: not showing respect

donate: to give something to an organization

elders: adults; people who are older than you

emergency: a dangerous situation that needs to be helped right away

environment: the indoor and outdoor world around you, including the places you live, play, and go to school, the air you breathe, the water you swim in and drink, and the soil that grows food

fable: a story that has been told for a long time; a fable usually teaches a lesson

fair: similar for everyone; when you're fair, you do your best to share, take turns, and treat each person with respect

fairness: treating other people the way you would like to be treated; giving everyone the kinds of rights and chances you have

family: the person or people you live with; people in families love and take care of each other

forgive: to give up hurt or angry feelings toward someone

forgiveness: the act of forgiving someone; giving up hurt or anger toward someone

foster children: children who don't live with the parents they're born or adopted to; they live with other families temporarily until they can return home or until another family is found for them

foster parents: adults who take children into their families temporarily until the children can return home or until another family is found for them

friend: someone you care about and like to do things with

genuine: real; when you're genuine, you don't pretend to be what you're not—you let people know the real *you*

graffiti: letters, names, words, or pictures drawn on walls or doors

honest: truthful; able to be trusted; when you're honest, you tell the truth and let people know the real you

honesty: truthfulness

instinct: the voice inside you that tells you when something does or doesn't feel right or safe; a "gut feeling"

jealous: feeling bad because someone has something you want; wishing you could have what someone else has or be like someone else

lobby: to show or tell your lawmakers how you want them to vote

log: a kind of list, diary, or journal that keeps track of when something happened

mosque: a Muslim place of worship

patriotic: feeling and showing love for your country

peso: a type of money used in Mexico and other Spanish-speaking countries

property: something owned by a person or group of people

recorder: a person who writes down the important things talked about during a meeting

relationship: the connection or tie you have to another person, such as a friend or family member

respect: care and concern for others and yourself; when you respect someone, you care about the person's ideas, thoughts, and feelings

responsibility: the act of making good choices, being dependable, and taking charge of your own actions, words, and thoughts

responsible: dependable; able to be counted on

role-play: to act out

safe: free from harm or risk

safety: being free from harm or risk

service: a kind act that you do for people, animals, or the environment

stress: worry that won't go away and that makes you feel bad

stroke: a sudden loss of blood to the brain

trustworthy: able to be counted on to do what you say you'll do; dependable

vicious: dangerously violent

violence: doing things that hurt people

violent: harmful; hurtful

Index

About the Author

Barbara A. Lewis is a national award-winning author and educator who teaches kids how to think and solve real problems. Her past students at Jackson Elementary in Salt Lake City, Utah, worked to clean up dangerous waste, improve sidewalks, plant thousands of trees, and fight crime. They lobbied and pushed through several laws in the Utah legislature and an amendment to a national law. The kids earned many national awards, including two President's Environmental Youth Awards, the Arbor Day Award, the Renew America Award, and the A Pledge and a Promise Environmental Award.

Stories about Barbara and her work have appeared in many national newspapers, magazines, and news programs, including *Newsweek, The Wall Street Journal, Family Circle*, "CBS This Morning," "CBS World News," and CNN. She has also written many articles and short stories for national magazines. Barbara's other books for Free Spirit Publishing include *A Leader's Guide to Being Your Best, What Do You Stand For?, Kids with Courage, The Kid's Guide to Service Projects, The Kid's Guide to Social Action,* and *The Survival Guide for Teachers of Gifted Kids* (with Jim Delisle). Her books have won Parenting's Reading-Magic Award and have been named "Best of the Best for Children" by the American Library Association, among other honors.

Barbara has lived in Indiana, New Jersey, Switzerland, Belgium, and Poland. She is the former Coordinator for PATHS (Program for Academically Talented and High-Achieving Students) in the Park City School District. She and her husband, Larry, are currently on a three-year service project in Eastern Europe where they are helping and teaching children and their families.

Other Great Books from Free Spirit

A Leader's Guide to Being Your Best
Character Building for Kids 7–10
by Barbara A. Lewis
Activities, questions, and handouts reinforce and expand the messages of the children's book. Together the two books comprise a complete starter course on character building. Includes reproducible handout masters. For grades 2–5.
$19.95; 128 pp.; softcover; 8½" x 11"

Being Your Best Character Stickers
$2.95; 100 stickers on 5 sheets; each sticker ⅜" x 2⅜"

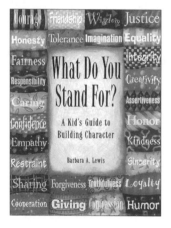

What Do You Stand For?
A Kid's Guide to Building Character
by Barbara A. Lewis
This book empowers children and teens to identify and build character traits. Inspiring quotations, activities, true stories, and resources make this book timely, comprehensive, and fun. For ages 11 & up.
$19.95; 284 pp.; softcover; B&W photos and illus.; 8½" x 11"

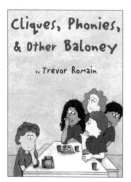

Cliques, Phonies, & Other Baloney
by Trevor Romain
Written for every kid who has ever felt excluded or trapped by a clique, this book blends humor with practical advice as it tackles a serious subject. For ages 8–13.
$9.95; 136 pp.; softcover; illus.; 5⅛" x 7"

Stick Up for Yourself!

Every Kid's Guide to Personal Power
and Positive Self-Esteem
Revised and Updated
by Gershen Kaufman, Ph.D., Lev Raphael, Ph.D.,
and Pamela Espeland
Realistic, encouraging, how-to advice for kids
on being assertive, building relationships,
becoming responsible, growing a "feelings
vocabulary," making good choices, solving
problems, setting goals, and more.
For ages 8–12.
$11.95; 128 pp.; softcover; illus.; 6" x 9"

A Teacher's Guide to Stick Up for Yourself!

A 10-Part Course in Self-Esteem
and Assertiveness for Kids
Revised and Updated
by Gershen Kaufman, Ph.D., Lev Raphael, Ph.D.,
and Pamela Espeland
Reinforces and expands the messages of the
student book with a step-by-step curriculum
in ten easy-to-use sessions. For teachers,
grades 3–7.
$19.95; 128 pp.; softcover; 8½" x 11"

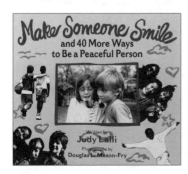

Make Someone Smile and 40 More Ways to Be a Peaceful Person

by Judy Lalli, M.S.,
photographs by Douglas L. Mason-Fry
Simple words and warm, appealing black-and-
white photographs present clear and under-
standable ideas for being a peaceful person
and promoting peaceful thoughts and behav-
iors. The photographs feature children of
many races modeling the skills of peacemak-
ing and conflict resolution in their everyday
lives. For all ages.
$9.95; 80 pp.; softcover; B&W photos; 8¼" x 7¼"

It's All in Your Head
A Guide to Understanding Your Brain
and Boosting Your Brain Power
by Susan L. Barrett
An "owner's manual" on the brain, written
especially for kids, this upbeat, engaging
book is for anyone who wants to know
more about the possibilities, mysteries,
and capabilities of the brain.
For ages 9–14.
$10.95; 160 pp.; softcover; illus.; 6" x 9"

You're Smarter Than You Think
A Kid's Guide to Multiple Intelligences
by Thomas Armstrong, Ph.D.
In clear, simple language, this book intro-
duces Howard Gardner's theory of multiple
intelligences. Kids learn how they can use
all eight intelligences in school, expand on
them at home, and draw on them to plan
for the future. Resources point the way to
books, software, games, and organizations
that can help kids develop the eight intelligences. Recommended for all kids, their
parents, and educators. For ages 8–12.
$15.95; 192 pp.; softcover; illus.; 7" x 9"

The Kid's Guide to Service Projects
Over 500 Service Ideas for Young People
Who Want to Make a Difference
by Barbara A. Lewis
Projects range from simple things anyone
can do to large-scale commitments that
involve whole communities. Choose from a
variety of topics including animals, crime,
the environment, literacy, politics, and
more. "Service Project How-Tos" offer
step-by-step instructions for creating flyers,
petitions, and press releases; fundraising;
and more. For ages 10 & up.
$12.95; 184 pp.; softcover; 6" x 9"